Guillermo Kuitca · burning beds

Little figures floating around murky gray interiors overwhelmed by the scale of their surroundings. Each room, a detailed description of an intolerable microcosm. The only escape... a bed.

With the weight of ourselves, the mattress becomes our body. Bones frame out its structure, and a labyrinth of veins and arteries chart out its flesh in search of yet another location to settle, cradled here, in sleep, we patch up our failures, speak with the dead, find community.

Flying over Mexico City reminds me that this is Earth I know. I can smell it by looking at it, All is remembered.

New neighborhoods explode, girdling every direction. The last address of memory is indistinguishable. Streets used to be named, from a proud and distinguished list, now they lie there with words forever untitled.

But from this vantage point you are safe, the rocket man, blasting through a virtual world unaware of even flying until you remember these vehicles often come crashing from the sky. Jesus, what a paranoid, your epitaph will read "I told you so".

Not to worry, the cradle lies below. These are your people and their communion is your medicine. And anyway this whole thing was dreamt up in bed.

Ray Smith

Guillermo Kuitca
burning beds
A Survey 1982 - 1994

Contemporary Art Foundation Amsterdam

Wexner Center for the Arts
Columbus, Ohio

Contemporary Art Foundation Amsterdam
concept

Center for the Fine Arts
Miami, Florida

Eduardo Lipschutz-Villa
curator

Whitechapel Art Gallery
London, United Kingdom

Sabien Ebeling Koning
coordination

Tel Aviv Museum of Art
Tel Aviv, Israel

We would like to
acknowledge the support
given to us by:

Sonia Becce
Fernando Bustillo
Ilja Devers
Meghan Ferrill
Kees Fopma
Lisa Fisher
Jane Friesen
Sherri Geldin
Claudio Gonzales Landa
Nehama Guralnik
Dirk Kleiman
Catherine Lampert
David Leiber
David Levine
Martin Loquet
Gustavo Lowry
Anetta Massie
Joost Meerman
Miguel Miguel
Jorge Miño
Mariana Oberzstern
Karen Polack
Kate Rawlinson
Sarah Rogers
Jill Rowe
Julie Shevach
Bob Simon
Rita Sitnick
Gian Enzo Sperone
Angela Westwater
Heather White

ISBN 90-73170-04-4

Lynne Cooke

Josefina Ayerza

Donald Baechler

Douglas Blau

John Coffey

Lelia Driben

Martin Filler

Jesús Fuenmayor

Louis Grachos

Marvin Heiferman

Anne Horton

Fabián Lebenglik

Lisa Liebmann

Marc Mayer

Charles Merewether

Miguel Miguel

Edith Newhall

Marcelo Pacheco

Alan Pauls

Robert Rainwater

Martin Rejtman

Sarah Rogers

Robert Rosenblum

Jerry Saltz

Allan Schwartzman

Edward Shaw

Ray Smith

Edward Sullivan

Alisa Tager

Richard Tuttle

Meyer Vaisman

Matthew Weinstein

Lynn Zelevanski

Contents

Walking into his studio one morning, all I could manage was, "He's burned the beds". Suddenly, they had gone up in flames. What was the conceptual intent of the bed, now these beds in flames? Burning is an act of demise, after all. Guillermo Kuitca's work has always sent me in search of answers, some salve for anxiety. Coded questions that demand decoding.

In this exhibition, Kuitca's work communicates a new self-assurance: it is mature. I have made a selection of paintings and drawings from early, pivotal moments in his career that force dialogue with the recent, more conceptually sophisticated work. The questions he poses are as abundant as ever.

When I left the studio that morning, I knew that the exhibition and this publication would be aptly named *Burning Beds. Guillermo Kuitca, Burning Beds: A Survey 1982-1994* will travel to different parts of the world. This publication will accompany the work.

I am grateful to Lynne Cooke who, by commitment and perseverance, allowed us to deliberately set-up an exchange through letters with Kuitca. What follows for the reader is a voyeuristic participation in intimate dialogue, one that illuminates the inner space of Kuitca and his work and of the process of art-making in general.

I selected works to disperse among a specific group of people who I thought could interact in a reactive manner to a specific piece, and to leave us in turn with a brief record of this exchange: a collected audience responding to individual, select works. Lynne Cooke and this generous network of thinking minds each contributed an essential brick on which this book was built.

I am thankful of the support and abundant energy of Angela Westwater and the staff of the Sperone Westwater Gallery, to Sabien Ebeling Koning and Hens Breet, who respectively in Amsterdam and New York, carried the weight of this project, and always to Sonia Becce in Buenos Aires.

The travel of this work would not be possible without the serious enthusiasm and commitment on the part of many professionals and the institutions they represent. I am extremely thankful to: Sherri Geldin, Director of the Wexner Center for the Arts; Sarah Rogers, Curator for the Wexner Center; Kate Rawlinson, Curator of the Center for Fine Arts in Miami; Catherine Lampert, Director of the Whitechapel Art Gallery; and Nehama Guralnik, Curator of the Tel Aviv Museum of Art.

I am deeply grateful to the many lenders who willingly entrusted the works of Kuitca for inclusion in this exhibition.

And lastly, to Guillermo Kuitca, for permitting complete access to his world. The next time I saw him after that morning, he was dancing on the canvas. *Naked Tango (after Warhol), 1994* was in progress and the studio, alive, burning beds in the distance.

Eduardo Lipschutz-Villa
New York City 1994

A mere two months prior to the publication of this catalogue and the première of Guillermo Kuitca's retrospective at the Wexner Center for the Arts, a terrorist bomb in his "native" city of Buenos Aires destroyed the principal cultural and community center for Argentina's 300,000 Jews. In addition to killing nearly 100 people and wounding many more, the blast obliterated much of the single largest archive of Judaica in Latin America. Documenting a century of Jewish presence in Argentina, this trove of books, documents comprised the "legacy of a community that for 100 years has struggled to be 'unmistakably Argentine' as (author Jorge Luis) Borges put it." [1]

My acquaintance with Guillermo Kuitca and my admiration for his work immediately cast upon this otherwise anonymous event an urgent and particularized dimension not shared by other, even more massive atrocities competing for media attention and, ultimately, for a seemingly diminished pool of global resources, will and ingenuity to ameliorate or resolve them. Because Buenos Aires happens to be the place that Kuitca calls "home" and because he is the descendent of Russian Jewish immigrants, this attack was instantly transformed from yet another faceless saga of horror among so many each day in The New York Times to a poignant personalized drama. Along with concern for Kuitca's own safety and that of his family and friends, my thoughts quickly leapt to the wrenching irony of the situation. This remarkable artist — whose principle themes are of memory and loss, home and displacement, personal identity and collective ethos — suddenly confronted by the very demons he frequently invokes, only this time summoned not by his own creative powers, but by a malevolent and uncontrollable force loose upon the land. Here yet another brutal reminder of the fragility of communal ties and the life-long (in fact, multi-generational) sentence cast upon the "outsider," no matter how deftly assimilated.

How might this public drama, so intimately entangled with Kuitca's private story, manifest itself in a body of work already rife with the haunting spectre of dispossession, banishment and endless roaming? There has always been about this art an aura of the untethered and floating in a place where boundaries, scale and compass points have no real meaning. With his tendency toward airborne perspectives, Kuitca sometimes reminds me of Wim Wenders' fallen angel who, tired of hovering chastely overhead, drops to earth with inevitable trials and tragedies. And for all his puckish ebullience, the work seems laden with the sobering wisdom of several lifetimes. "Nobody forgets anything," the title for one series of paintings, might well describe Kuitca's personal creed in which memory is both blessing and curse. Indeed, while that explosion a few months ago may well have "left a gaping hole in the Argentine imagination," (Ibid.) one readily presumes that at least one local artist has already begun the process of reclamation.

The Wexner Center is honored to inaugurate the exhibition "Burning Beds Guillermo Kuitca: A Survey 1982-1994." It has been a supreme pleasure to work with esteemed colleague and curator Eduardo Lipschutz-Villa, whose passion for Kuitca's work is matched by exquisite comprehension, as amply demonstrated in this and previous projects. I express my heartfelt thanks to the entire Board and staff of the Wexner Center for their many contributions to the exhibition's realization, and my special appreciation to the Ohio Arts Council for its magnificent support of this presentation. It is our utmost good fortune to welcome Guillermo Kuitca to the Wexner Center and to Columbus. He is an exceptionally gifted artist whose abundant talents we are proud to share with this community.

Sherri Geldin
Director
Wexner Center for the Arts
Columbus, Ohio

[1] (Edna Aizenberg, "Alongside the Dead in Argentina"; The New York Times, August 2, 1994).

The presentation of Guillermo Kuitca's work at the Tel Aviv Museum of Art, the first comprehensive exhibition of a contemporary Argentine artist ever to take place in Israel, fulfills a reciprocal desire between artist and institution. As a Latin American artist of growing international renown, and as a Jew, concerned with the idea of locale and displacement, whose work plots out the geographical nowhere that is at the same time the spiritual everywhere – Kuitca's work will prove to be very meaningful to the Israeli public, who might conceptually encounter through this work some of the same anxieties which previous generations have passed on to this new society.

Kuitca's metaphorical work, charged with highly symbolic meanings, gives expression to private as well as collective memories, longings, alienation and anxieties. It is both autobiographical and universal, tied to the specific history of his native land and to the existential state of life in the *Galuth* – the diaspora.

Communicating through this exhibition the wide spectrum of his artistic language, Kuitca's work will allow us to enter the symbiotic world of literature, theatre, and poetry, whose powerful visual associations allow confrontation with the various levels of our own reality.

Nehama Guralnik
Tel Aviv Museum of Art

In a professional sense Kuitca has had hardly any visibility in Britain. However, as with many other distant places, he has made ties of his own. There are paintings describing generic Victorian street plans; there are texts and images which escalate the vocabulary and the irony which the uninhibited confessional imagery of Francis Bacon and Gilbert and George have inspired; and there are titles and sentiments that play with the Beatles' lyrics. In turn, in this country those following contemporary art in the eighties received the mythology that surrounded this Argentinian artist (b. 1961) who began exhibiting at the age of thirteen. Waiting until 1995 to show Kuitca has the advantage of coinciding with his own decision to re-enter themes he began in the early '80s, not least new and mysterious paintings using mirage-like stage settings and others built on unnervingly reduced plans, stadiums and theatres as well as apartments.

The Whitechapel hopes that by presenting in depth his work of the last ten years, Kuitca can be seen in the context of other painters, like Tony Bevan and Miquel Barcelo, who have been shown at the Gallery recently. We also anticipate that by considering the ideas and sensibility present in the work we will strengthen our knowledge of what has been happening in Latin America, a process that began at the Whitechapel with exhibitions like Helio Oiticica in 1969 and continued with Kahlo, Tunga and Jaar, and has been mirrored in other British independent galleries.

We are very indebted to Eduardo Lipschutz-Villa and the Contemporary Art Foundation Amsterdam for suggesting this exhibition, (and its title!), to the Wexner Center for the Arts in Ohio where it was first seen and to Lynne Cooke for a characteristically original and scholarly consideration of the artist and the art. The generous support of the Cultural Affairs Department of the Ministry of Foreign Affairs of Argentina allowed us to participate in this ambitious gathering of some of Kuitca's most important work. Our gratitude extends equally to the lenders and particularly to Kuitca himself.

Catherine Lampert
Director
Whitechapel Art Gallery

15 July 1994 **ITERATIONS** 10 October 1994

Letters: Lynne Cooke · Guillermo Kuitca

15 July 1994 Unfortunately, due to difficulties with the immigration department, I am not at present free to travel, and so cannot visit you in Buenos Aires as planned prior to writing a text for the catalogue for your exhibition at the Wexner Center, in Columbus, this fall.

I am really sorry because I'd been much looking forward to spending time with you, to being in the studio, and to experiencing something of the wider context in which you work. Lacking that makes me very hesitant about embarking on an essay, as I don't feel I have a sufficient grasp of the situation, nor have we spent enough time talking together to make me confident of the ground on which I would hazard an interpretation.

I therefore would like to suggest an alternative: a fax dialogue. By this I mean that we should exchange letters by fax over the next few months. I hope that the course we follow will be open-ended and even unexpected, with more musings and speculations than would be possible in a spoken interview.

Does this seem an acceptable proposal to you? I realize in suggesting it I am putting much of the burden back on you. It should, however, result in something more revealing and closer to your concerns. I look forward to hearing from you.

18 July 1994 The news that you will not be able to come to Buenos Aires made me sad but I am glad that you will find a way to keep going with the project.

Writing is not my best, specially in English but I agree with you that this kind of dialogue fits very well into the purpose of the book.

You said in your first fax that you preferred not to use the question and answer system but it would be easier for me if you could include some more specific questions with the general issues.

I look forward to beginning our dialogue.

30 July 1994 Sorry for the delay in replying to you. I've been thinking about a way of beginning and realize that wherever we begin does not have to be the beginning; we can rearrange the bits afterwards. Also we can always go back and make minor changes if that seems necessary.

Please don't worry about your English. That, too, can be revised or corrected, if necessary, at a later stage.

What I hoped to do was to write not single questions and answers but rather some thoughts and for you to respond in any way that you feel is appropriate.

Vermeer's *Art of Painting* is for Svetlana Alpers in her discussion of seventeenth century Dutch art a key work that "illuminates the resemblances between pictures and maps", in an era when there was an unparalleled "coincidence between mapping and picturing." She argues that the basis of this relationship is "a common notion of knowledge and the belief that it is to be gained and asserted through pictures". Many theorists have recently asserted that we are returning to a period in which visual languages, and, specifically, media representations are the prevailing sources of information, communication and knowledge, rather than language per se. At the same time we have become very familiar with the oft-repeated, if not altogether convincing, claim that painting is in a state of crisis, that its formerly crucial role in communication has been usurped, whatever remains of its expressive potential.

I'm very interested in the variety of ways that you have utilized cartography in your art, Guillermo. You seem to take the most commonplace forms of maps, namely, the street plan and the road map as your starting point, and then simply but subtly transform them. For example, in one painting all the names of the major cities included in the segment represented have been replaced with the name of a single town, one that belongs to another country. On another occasion the names of cities in one country have been interpolated into a fragment representing an entirely different nation. So what is designed to ensure that one finds one's way without error becomes its very antithesis, a guide that takes one to another place altogether, or better, to no place – which may be defined as utopia, or dystopia, perhaps. A somewhat different transformation seems to occur when the road maps are painted onto the surfaces of mattresses. The principal site of sleep, and with it of dreams (and nightmares), becomes the locus of the preeminent image of individual self-propelled travelling, that is, of driving. This conjunction produces a wonderful metaphorical image of a spatio-temporal voyaging that is not constrained by the literal and material, that belongs instead to the realm of dreaming and the unconscious.

To return, then, to Vermeer. In this painting the identity of the map maker and the painter is asserted by the fact that, uniquely in his art, Vermeer inscribes his own name on the map as its maker. Alpers

◄ *Johannes Vermeer*
The Art of Painting, c. 1665-1667
oil on canvas
120 x 100 cm. (47 1/4 x 39 3/8 in.)
Kunsthistorisches Museum, Vienna

points out, however, that Vermeer's claim to the identity of mapmaker is powerfully confirmed elsewhere in his oeuvre: "The only two male figures to whom he devoted entire paintings – the *Astronomer* ... and the *Geographer* ... were also by profession makers of maps and they encompassed the heavens and earth between them". She then continues: "If this map [in the *Art of Painting*] is presented like a painting, to what notion of painting does it correspond? Vermeer suggests an answer to this question", she contends, "in the form of the word 'descriptio' prominently written on the upper border of the map.... Map makers or publishers were referred to as 'world describers' and their maps or atlases as the worlds described.... The aim of Dutch painters was to capture on a surface a great range of knowledge and information about the world.... Like mappers they made additive works that could not be taken in from a single viewing point. Theirs was not a window on the Italian model of art but rather, like a map, a surface on which is laid out an assemblage of the world".

This passage was interesting to me when thinking of your work, partly because you might also be termed a "world describer", a map maker, geographer and astronomer, but it is not a literal, phenomenological world that you conjure. But partly, too, because I was curious about the ways that you have often had recourse, in other series of paintings, to what appear to be stage sets (which in themselves are other vehicles for the creation of fictitious or fantastical worlds), in favor of any straightforward imaging of the external world. In this way, as with the use of architectural plans in lieu of representations of buildings, there is constantly a presentation of the mechanisms, vehicles or filters by which worlds are described, and by implication, a discourse on how you view painting and its role.

3 August 1994 Lately I can see an almost straight line connecting the road maps, the city plans, the floor plans and the stage paintings, but every series of work starts as a vision rather than a project.

The image of a mad person contained in a room with soft walls crossed my mind when I started to work on the mattress paintings. Although the bed was a leitmotiv for so long in my pictures I guess I was fascinated by surfaces like the mattress with buttons used formerly to protect enraged people from hitting their heads against the walls. It was after that that I used the road maps. I might borrow images from films, as in many other works like the prisons.

The map with a repeated name of the same city was a kind of vision (a vision of The Obsession). I can see someone leaving a place and arriving at the same place and so on.

These adulterated or useless maps took me to Beuys, when he conceived the two pieces of a hammer as a vision of the pathetic. It was not even a broken hammer, it was nothing. I don't know Beuys's work so well, and I never saw that piece, I only heard about it a long time ago and I guess I wanted to bring his vision closer to my work.

With these paintings I was close to a definition of Trauma. Trauma always returns you to the same experience.

In many poems by Borges you can find the idea that a place is all places, a day all days and so on. He said in a poem called *James Joyce* something like this: in one day of a Man are the days of Time.

After your letter I can see a stage set as a "Surface on which is laid out an assemblage of the world", "like a Map".

22 August 1994 Please forgive my long delay in replying to your last fax. I've been travelling a great deal, most notably to the Côte d'Ivoire, and then to the west coast of Ireland. I was thinking a lot about what you wrote in your last letter about trauma and obsession, about always returning to the same place. And also about your citation from Borges, that one place is all places, that one day all days.

Everywhere I went people were taking photographs, and often the local people resident in those places were actively participating in the process, joining in, or at least, silently becoming complicit with it. The impulse to garner these images is less to have information about those places than to have proof that the person was actually there, inserted into the geography. In many ways it seems very similar to the impulse to trace over a map the route that one took, superimposing one's own trajectory over the skeletal road plan.

In your paintings depicting road maps or grids of city streets, there is a similar invitation to the viewer to insert a trajectory, to trace a path. To follow the map is to draw, at least hypothetically, a route, to journey. If the spatial has been subjected to a predetermined organization, the temporal remains open-ended. In imagining potential journeys the spectator effectively retraces your paths, and remarks part of the cartography. In this way time, as it were, thickens: it takes on flesh. And while there is no internal narrative integral to the map, its use always introduces one. Neither the time of history nor the contingencies of the present seems to be implied in this but rather the accumulation of experience inherent in meandering. This meditativeness prompts both a reflexive response to the painting, an engagement with its hermeneutics, and an invitation to reverie. Not, therefore, to the question of here and there,but of now and not-now.

27 August 1994   During this week I've been trying to think of something to keep our dialogue going but it is difficult to say something different from what you already said.

As with someone's journey through one of those paintings that I did with maps I can't find a way to get out of the same ideas and think about something that takes me to another place.

Will you suggest to me which road I should take?

Maybe something will come out. Thanks.

4 September 1994   I, too, am having some trouble finding the threads, or threading my way through the terrain, to mix a cartographic metaphor. Partly, it's a question of how to explore the issues that your work proposes rather than simply describing to you my responses to your art, which would leave you the possibility of agreeing or disagreeing with me, or of correcting my readings. Partly, its a matter of finding a vehicle that is not rhetorical but sufficiently elastic for you to take it in any direction you might choose.

I recently read a book by Stephen Hall called *Mapping the Next Millenium*, as I hoped it would introduce me to some ways of thinking about cartography that were new or topical, and that would focus beyond or outside issues of terrestrial geography. I was prompted, too, by the recognition that your maps are not literal plans: not only are other names substituted sometimes for the correct city names, but the places themselves must on occasion function for you more as imaginative locales rather than as actual sites; they must be resonant for the associations they generate with situations in, say, films or novels rather than with direct experience. At least, that is part of what I glean from the fact that often they are painted onto the surfaces of mattresses: they invite reverie, oneiric meanderings in place of analytic scrutiny.

In his book Hall argues that there is currently an explosion in the field and the discourses of map-making: a renaissance in exploration, he calls it, pointing to unprecedented studies of the ocean floor and of remote galaxies in outer space, as well as in genetics, physics and neuroscience. "The real breakthrough – messy and beyond category," he writes, "a chain reaction rather than a single explosion – is in twentieth century sciences's ability to measure, and therefore to map, a breathtaking range of spatial domains.... With stunningly precise new instruments of measurement developed over the last half century and with the tremendous graphic powers provided by computers over the last two decades, everyone from archaeologists to zoologists has been able to discover, explore, chart, and visualize physical domains so remote and fantastic that the effort involves nothing less than the reinvention of the idiom of geography". To demonstrate this he cites part of the definition of "map" given in the celebrated 1910 edition of the *Encyclopaedia Britannica*, once a benchmark in modern scholarship: "a representation, on a plane and a reduced scale, of part or whole of the earth's surface". From today's perspective, he argues, "That narrow land-based definition of map, like the geocentric myth of the earth itself, has been conceptually overwhelmed and ultimately retired by scientific advances since the end of World War II". And amongst those domains still being discovered and reconnoitered he mentions "chromosomes, zygotes, atomic surfaces, star forming regions of the Milky Way, the large scale galactic structures of the Universe".

For me, the book was, however, equally fascinating for the sense it gave that much new information gets coded and revealed in the guise of maps, albeit maps defined in the broadest terms, rather than as, say, figures, charts, or even diagrams. This preference for revealing new knowledge in primarily visual rather than verbal terms is very suggestive. Interestingly, often the subjects of the investigation are not seen directly but via the tracks they leave on light sensitive paper, or the bruises they make on an intermediary medium.

Unfortunately, virtually all the material he discussed was centered on data based quantifiable maps. It is only in the final couple of pages that he turns to other kinds of cartography. He briefly mentions the

Australian Aborigines who map their world through song-lines, which may be transformed into dream-paintings "so rich and precise in their geographic detail that they merge mythology and cartography". Acknowledging that mapping, knowledge and power are intricately interlinked Hall quotes from J. B. Harley's "definitive" *History of Cartography*: "The social history of maps, unlike that of literature, art or music, appears to have few genuinely popular, alternative or subversive modes of expression. Maps are pre-eminently a language of power not of protest". He then introduces Henry David Thoreau who, in the eighteenth century, questioned the value of certain forms of contemporary land exploration, seeing them as digressive, as diversions from an interior mapping of the self, which he, Thoreau, termed "home-cosmography". "It is easier to sail many thousands of miles through cold and storm and cannibals, in a government ship, with five hundred men and boys to assist one", Thoreau declares, "than it is to explore the private sea, the Atlantic and Pacific of one's being alone". And he counsels: "Be a Columbus to whole new continents and worlds within you, opening new channels not of trade but of thought". I imagine, Guillermo, that that might be a more fruitful analogue for confronting some of your work than any of the zones that Hall treks, bearing in mind Melville's claim that "true places" are never "down on any map". Yet if conjectural cartography does indeed guide your explorations why then do road maps and street plans, amongst the many forms available for roaming unknown or unfamiliar terrain, best serve your needs?
Looking forward to hearing from you,

8 September 1994 Yesterday I put together the installation of beds with maps painted on mattresses before they were packed up and sent to the United States for the exhibition at the Wexner Center. Since I had decided to send sixty instead of seventy-two beds, I had to decide which twelve would stay in Buenos Aires. According to what criteria, if any, should I undertake the selection?

Looking at them one at a time, I asked myself what I was looking for in taking one instead of another, and I remembered that from the beginning the places named in the maps didn't represent anything I knew, had seen in films, nor read in books; no here or there, just names. The name and its sound and resonance. I came across that word, resonance, in your last letter. In the maps with the name of one city repeated, there was no one coming or going, but rather someone saying that name, repeating it to himself time and time again. As much as I could, I avoided using the names of cities that have, for me, an excessively visual reference; you rarely read "Paris", "Chicago" or "Buenos Aires", in my paintings. When I began with the maps, I used road maps from Western Europe because, of the maps that were easy to get, they had the highest concentration of names, roads,highways; of references in general. So much so that it was hard to tell one name from another, and I liked that. That's why many of the works made between 1987-1989 have maps of Europe. With time, I came up with other variations, and now I think I prefer more legible maps; in a certain way, they have a purer sound.

Genealogical charts are the representation of a chain reaction. The genealogical charts that I painted are a chain reaction to my own painting. I wonder if Stephan Hall in his book mentions family maps and if there will be a new ability to measure or render genealogy or if there will be an element to measure and represent our memory, even though genealogical charts are based on what we know, not what we remember.

To have painted genealogical charts was a simple consequence of having painted maps. Again, the resonance of the names was essential; it is unlikely that we will meet these people, nevertheless the name is all we need to build the scene.

In the last chapter of a book that Bruce Chatwin and Paul Theroux wrote *Patagonia Revisited*, Chatwin cites an incredible poem written by John Donne in his death bed. Donne sees himself as a map lying on the bed in front of his doctors changed into cosmographers. The poem is the following:

> *Since I am coming to that holy room,*
> *Where, with thy choir of saints for evermore,*
> *I shall be made thy music; as I come*
> *I tune the instrument here at the door,*
> *And what I must do then, think here before.*

Whilst my physicians by their Love are grown
Cosmographers, and I their map, who lie
Flat on this bed, that by them may be shown
That this is my south-west discovery
Per fretum febris, by these straits to die,

I joy, That is these straits, I see my west;
For, though their currents yield return to none.

What shall my west hurt me? As west and east
In all flat maps (and I am one) are one,
So death doth touch the resurrection.

Is the Pacific Sea my home? Or are
the Eastern riches? Is Jerusalem?
Anyan, and Magellan, and Gibraltar,
All straits, are none but straits, are ways to them,
whether where Japhet dwelt, or Cham, or Shem.

We think that Paradise and Calvary,
Christ's Cross, and Adam's tree, stood in one place
Look Lord, and find both Adam's met in me;
As the first Adam's sweat surrounds my face,
May the last Adam's blood my soul embrace.

So, in his purple wrapped receive me Lord,
By these his thorns give his other crown;
And as to others' souls I preached thy word
Be this my text, my sermon to mine own,
Therefore that he may raise the Lord throws down.

The entire poem seems, at some remote point, a wonderful description of what I once tried to do in my works.

I hope to have the pleasure of reading your letters soon. Meanwhile, I'll keep thinking about the done and the said and trying, if only just once, to come out of my work.

11 September 1994 I was very struck by your comment about avoiding reference in relation to the names of cities in the paintings of road maps, and the potency of their sound for you. It made me wonder about the tendency, which I clearly share, to impute biographical meaning into your choice of subjects as well as into their rendering. And wonder, too, whether it was generated by this situation or merely exacerbated by it.

It occurred also in relation to your recent set of paintings of "ideal" building types, a group of works made by drawing "blueprints" of the buildings onto monochromatic pastel grounds. Notwithstanding their ideal and generic architectural typologies, these paintings recall Agnes Martin's work, to me, alongside that of certain French neoclassical architects, including Ledoux and Boullée. And for all the allusions which may be drawn via Foucault to notions of surveillance and power, these ethereal, diagrammatic forms are paradoxically fragile and evanescent, and, in this, markedly contrary to their built counterparts. In many other groups of your paintings, including a number which contain the image of the apartment plan, the improvisational technique reads metaphorically as a searching to find and fix a form: worked, layered surfaces, traces of pentimenti, are habitually so coded. By contrast, the diagrammatic floor plans on their delicate unblemished surfaces bear no sense of the tentative, and of making and unmaking, for all their obviously hand-drawn character. Consequently they seem to exist in a pure state, outside the contingencies and particularities of time, site, locale and history. This is, in turn, reinforced by the ways in which light seems to glance off the surfaces. It never penetrates the thin membrane of skin, whereas light in many of the other paintings emerges from within, seeping through the seams between layers of differently textured pigment. The resulting suspension and dislocation of these images has, nonetheless, for me a significant relation with the paintings of maps and streetplans in that since they are always fragments of some larger entity and devoid of beginning or end, of coordinates or origination for destination, they, too, ultimately proffer a suspended state.

One of the striking features about the writing on your art is how seldom issues of place and cultural location enter into it – aside, that is, from the almost mandatory reference to Borges, who must be the best known and most revered of Argentine artists of the twentieth century. I think I remember you once saying to me that you did not want your work to be thought of in nationalistic terms, and that you resisted any tendency to be made somehow to represent your country, or to stand for a particular cultural identity.

Earlier this week I read an essay by Himani Bannerji in a catalogue called, tellingly, *Beyond Destination*. She analyses the traps and pressures resulting from a subtle but relentlessly inescapable racism that seems to cause contemporary immigrants and exiles in western countries to adopt the trappings, the cultural shards of "home", and to rely on these insignia – "trivia assembled into constellations of meaning" – to indicate difference and, with it, a form of identity. For her, such "traditions are not of a whole cloth". She contends "they are invented from bits and pieces, from parental cultural baggage,... from music listened to on cassettes, and from...films.... Not much comes from reading, since written materials lacks the perfect emptiness and malleability of the visual image and of echoed sound."

"Why do we want to be 'authentic' so badly? What makes us think that an existence at any given moment is anything but authentic? ", she concludes rhetorically, before answering her own question: "Being always has a content, a form, a room and a reason in history, in daily life, and in desire. Yet this simple truth is so often overridden..." In a sense by characterising your work as I did at the beginning of this letter, as in various ways suspending destinations, or proposing immaterial sites and fictive situations in the theater-like scenarios, I may have answered my own question as to where you stand on these issues. On the other hand I may once again be imputing biographical meaning to issues that remain for you more abstract.

I hope this is not too vague, Guillermo. It seems an important issue to touch on, though I may have introduced it in rather an artificial way.

13 September 1994   Visibility is a trap.

With this Foucault sums up the principle of the Panopticon. I associate my work with the panoptic vision. A gaze that sees all. In many of my paintings I construct a panoptic viewer even without using a panoptic plan. The same happens in the stage paintings and in the house plans: everything is exposed to the viewer's eye. I like the idea of Ricardo Bofill that says each construction is a monument, each public space a theater.

While the map paintings become family maps and thus more private, the family houses become ideal types, thus more public.

The *Tablada Suite* came out of the apartment plan paintings. Now I can see all the suite painted on the pastel walls of the rooms in the apartment. I also see a place for each of us, a very specific one in the *Tablada Suite* paintings: A seat, a bed, a tombstone, a cell. In these works I used graphite and acrylic on canvas. More important than the materials themselves was the way I used the graphite, leaving marks of the making. But most important was the use of the glossy varnish, at once unifying the graphite and the acrylic and separating the painting from the viewer in the sense that Francis Bacon did by always putting glass over his paintings. While these paintings are so heavily varnished that they can be washed, the dirtiness is eternal.

> *If (as the Greek asserts in the Cratylus),*
> *The name is archetype of the thing,*
> *The rose is in the letters of "rose"*
> *and the length of the Nile is "Nile".*
> from *The Golem.*

I am afraid that I had to go back to Borges.

The fact that I choose places because of their names doesn't mean that those choices aren't personal (if I understand "biographical" to mean personal). This is what Carlos Fuentes said about Buenos Aires:

"...To know Buenos Aires is to know that perhaps no other city in the world cries out more strongly – verbalize me!

An old joke says that Mexicans are descendants of the Aztecs, Peruvians of the Incas and Argentinians of the boats. A city without history ... Buenos Aires has to name itself to itself to know it exists." He continues, "The language of the Argentines is a response to the demands of a city that wants to be verbalized to affirm its phantasmagorical being ... Is there anything more Argentine than the need verbally to fill the empty places calling on all the libraries in the world to fill the blank book of Argentina?"

I am leaving on Friday, keep sending faxes to the same number. After the 26th of September I will be in Columbus, Ohio and after that, from the first of October in New York where I hope to talk to you, which might be strange after all this writing.

23 September 1994   I realize that now you have left your home it will be difficult to continue in this manner, and that once we meet in New York at the end of the month it will in some ways break the "spell", and so perhaps this should be my last letter.

I am sorry because I have found this a fascinating project, partly because it led to a way of thinking that for me would not have been possible in a one-to-one interview, but more because it kept my train of thought very actively in dialogue with you rather than free to roam as is the case in writing an essay. It has a kind of simultaneous distance that sometimes emboldens me to ask questions or propose hypotheses that would not always be easy to pose directly to you, and yet it has an immediacy and informality somewhat different from letter writing. If this is what information highway promises then I greatly welcome it!

I had considered reading back over our correspondence before writing this last, to see if it was appropriate to summarise, or to fill in missing gaps, but on reflection, I think that it should stand in its cumulative fashion, and that I'll end with one large question. What does it mean for you to be an artist? (I could break this down by asking who you work for, what you feel are the responsibilities, if any, of an artist today, and related questions, but it's a rather impertinent or, if not, importunate query so I'll leave it for you to reply, if you wish to reply, in any vein you choose.) I very much look forward to seeing you in New York.

28 September 1994   I am not sure what an artist is. Maybe I never chose to be an artist. I have painted since I was a little child and I don't have memories of myself not being a painter. I do have memories of how art affected me. At home we had a collection of periodicals called *Pinacoteca de los Genios*, which included masterpieces from every period in the history of art. For me names like Picasso, Van Gogh and Kandinsky were Argentine and they didn't have any different attributes from the ones I had.

It didn't take much to realize these artists were 'geniuses' and an abyss separated me from each if them. The first time I faced this fact was when an exhibition called *De Cézanne à Miro*, came to Buenos Aires. This was in 1966 or 1967. Like in Fellini's *Amacord* we all ran to see this once in a lifetime event. Even though this show was from the collection of The Museum of Modern Art in New York, I believed everything came from France. At night I prayed not to die before knowing Paris.

My ideas of art was changing with the time, from very ambitious to less ambitious ideas, from clear to more vague and even vaguer ideas.

Although intuition is for me a most important thing, I feel a personal responsibility, which I try not to impose on other artists, which is to comment in my works on the human condition; to try to say something on that. To give order to everything that surrounds me. To try to understand the world in which I live. To assume myself incapable of understanding why, so I can look for an answer.

Like other artists, I would like the people in front of my work to ask questions about themselves and not about me. I want each to know about himself or herself and not only about me. But generally, I feel ridiculous if I think of the effect my work will cause or if I try to manipulate some kind of particular reaction.

Through the years I have collected perfect metaphors of art, founded in fragments of songs, films or poems, in anecdotes or quotes from daily live, to use when the occasion arises. But I am far from home and your question surprised me in this hotel in Columbus, Ohio. I don't have anything in my head. I am sitting in front of this enormous window, looking all over the city. Everything out there seems to beg: "Decipher me", to demand: "Make me better, darker, simple, bolder ... Make me whatever, but yours."

Now I pray, take me back home.

I will be in New York from October 2nd-8th and I will be happy to meet you.

10 October 1994

Following our conversation in New York yesterday, a postscript seems in order.

I'm not surprised to learn that you feel no particular connection to the work of Agnes Martin: I hadn't really supposed that you would. Rather, what I was trying to probe was something to do with the ways in which the *Tablada Suite* works very differently from most of your other paintings. The diagrammatical character of the outline drawing, the iconic images which are almost gridlike on occasion, and the very flat surfaces with their high gloss finish, imbue these works with a different kind of light and presence from your other works. And, for all that traces of their making remain in the occasional blurring of the graphite lines, they have a kind of remoteness, and distance, very different in character from the immediacy that the worked surfaces impart in the other paintings, whose imagery often appears as fragments or parts of a larger entity. I therefore felt they had a different heritage.

I was also aware, as you pointed out, that I had ducked the question of genealogies, and that, as you supposed, Hall did not discuss them in his text. Family trees, of the kind one finds as a student in history books, always seemed to me marvelous in their reduction of the mess that typifies most family relations to clear schematic tables. Pedigree and lineage today seem grand notions for the intimacy and complexity that generally marks family connections. From the books I have at hand I could not find instances of the ways in which other cultures have envisioned such relationships, though I have a vague memory that in some Polynesian societies these are embodied in the weaving of certain baskets.

I began this dialogue with reference to Vermeer, but would like to finish with one of the most enchanting maps imaginable and beloved of many children, that of the Bellman in Lewis Carroll's *Hunting of the Snark*:

> He had brought a large map representing the sea,
> Without the least vestige of land,
> And the crew were much pleased when they found it to be
> A map they could all understand.
> "What's the good of Mercator's North Poles and Equators,
> Tropics, Zones, and Meridian Lines?"
> So the Bellman would cry: and the crew would reply
> "They are merely conventional signs!
> "Other maps are such shapes, with their islands and capes!
> But we've got our brave captain to thank"
> (So the crew would protest)
> "that he's brought us the best –
> A perfect and absolute blank!"

Thanks very much for your willingness to engage in this process, Guillermo.

Works on Paper, 1981-1993
mixed media
variable dimensions
collection of the artist
courtesy Sperone Westwater, New York

Nadie Olvida Nada, 1982
acrylic on hardboard
variable dimensions
collection of the artist
courtesy Sperone Westwater, New York

Mi Hijo Es Bello Como el Sol, 1982
acrylic on wood
42 x 191 cm. (16 1/2 x 75 1/4 in.)
collection of the artist
courtesy Sperone Westwater, New York

Yo, Como el Angel, 1985
acrylic and oil on canvas
189 x 320 cm. (24 1/2 x 126 in.)
collection Jorge and Marion Helft, Buenos Aires

El Mar Dulce, 1984
acrylic on paper and canvas
170 x 310 cm. (67 x 122 in.)
collection Sonia Becce, Buenos Aires

La Busca de la Felicidad, 1985
acrylic on canvas
118 x 193 cm. (46 1/2 x 75 3/4 in.)
collection of the artist
courtesy Sperone Westwater, New York

Si Yo Fuera el Invierno Mismo, 1985
acrylic on canvas
125 x 195 cm. (49 1/2 x 76 3/12 in.)
collection Humberto Ugobono, San Juan, Puerto Rico

Siete Ultimas Canciones, 1986
acrylic on canvas
131 x 201.9 cm. (51 1/2 x 79 1/2 in.)
courtesy of the Bacardi Art Foundation

Siete Ultimas Canciones, 1986
acrylic on canvas
140 x 170 cm. (55 x 67 in.)
collection Juan Cristobal Rautenstrauch, Buenos Aires

Si Yo Fuera el Invierno Mismo, 1986
acrylic on canvas
137 x 190 cm. (54 x 74 3/4 in.)
collection Jorge and Marion Helft, Buenos Aires

Si Yo Fuero el Invierno Mismo, 1986
acrylic on canvas
110 x 252 cm. (55 1/2 x 99 1/4 in.)
collection Javier Benitez, Monterrey

Planta Con Texto, 1989
acrylic and oil on canvas
200 x 140 cm. (78 3/4 x 55 1/4 in.)
collection of the artist
courtesy Sperone Westwater, New York

Coming, 1989
acrylic on canvas
237 x 237 cm. (93 1/4 x 93 1/4 in.)
collection Jorge and Marion Helft, Buenos Aires

Corona de Espinas, 1990
acrylic and oil on canvas
150 x 200 cm. (78 3/4 x 59 in.)
collection Joost Lagerwey, Amsterdam

L'Enfance du Christ, 1990
acrylic on canvas
203 x 230 cm. (80 x 126 in.)
collection Aurelio Lopéz-Rocha, Mexico

Untitled, 1991
acrylic on canvas
229 x 198 cm. (90 1/8 x 78 in.)
collection Carlos and Rosa de la Cruz, Miami

San Juan, 1991
acrylic on canvas
195 x 170 cm. (76 3/4 x 67 in.)
Private collection

Untitled, 1991
acrylic on canvas
198 x 283 cm. (78 x 111 1/2 in.)
collection Moisés and Diana Berezdivin, San Juan, Puerto Rico
Untitled, 1991

mixed media on canvas
214 x 192 cm. (96 x 74 3/4 in.)
collection of the artist
courtesy Sperone Westwater, New York

Coming Home, 1992
acrylic on canvas
198 x 188 cm. (78 x 74 in.)
collection Josefina Ayerza, New York

Untitled, 1992
oil on mattress
200 x 200 cm. (80 x 80 in.)
collection Patricia Phelps de Cisneros, Caracas

Nordrhein, 1992
oil on matttress
198 x 198 cm. (79 x 79 in.)
collection PaineWebber Group Inc., New York

Untitled, 1992
acrylic on canvas
282 x 373 cm. (111 x 146 3/4 in.)
collection of the artist
courtesy Sperone Westwater, New York

The Tablada Suite II, 1991
graphite and acrylic on canvas
190 x 160 cm. (75 x 63 in.)
collection Carlos and Rosa de la Cruz, Miami, Florida

The Tablada Suite V, 1992
graphite and acrylic on canvas
181 x 126 cm. (71 1/4 x 49 1/2 in.)
private collection

Untitled, 1992
mixed media on canvas
165 x 155 cm. (64 3/4 x 61 1/4 in.)
collection of the artist
courtesy Sperone Westwater, New York

Untitled, 1993
mixed media on canvas
190 x 190 cm. (75 x 75 in.)
collection David Meitus, Chicago
courtesy Sperone Westwater, New York

Corona de Espinas, 1993
oil on canvas
198 x 288 cm. (78 x 113 1/2 in.)
collection Ron and Ann Pizzutti, Ohio

People on Fire, 1993
mixed media on canvas
193 x 280 cm. (76 x 110 in.)
collection North Carolina Museum of Art, Raleigh
purchased with funds from various donors by exchange

People on Fire, 1993
mixed media on canvas
196 x 298 cm. (77 1/4 x 117 1/4 in.)
collection of the artist
courtesy Sperone Westwater, New York

Installation, 1993
acrylic on mattress (60)
size variable
collection of the artist
courtesy Sperone Westwater, New York

Untitled, 1994
oil and acrylic on canvas
195 x 235 cm. (76 3/4 x 92 1/2 in.)
collection Mark and Nedra Oren, Florida

Untitled, 1994
acrylic on canvas
199 x 189 cm. (78 1/2 x 74 1/2 in.)
collection Ron and Ann Pizzutti, Ohio

Naked Tango (after Warhol), 1994
acrylic on canvas
195.5 x 148 cm. (76 7/8 x 58 3/8 in.)
collection of the artist
courtesy Sperone Westwater, New York

A Survey 1982 -1994

Confronting Kuitca's work takes us into
the pain of his system. As his own witness, Kuitca provides us early on with
his first commentaries. From that
moment of detachment, he originates
the code of order for his world, an
attempt to organize the chaos that
reigns outside his studio.

Forget provenance.

Kuitca's work appears at first with such
elegance and virtuosity that the senses
are quickly satiated by pure beauty
alone. Consider this the ease, the entry,
into the conceptual process of the work
that takes you to new levels of involve-
ment.

Forget virtuosity.

ELV

Untitled, 1994
oil and acrylic on canvas
195 x 235 cm. (76 3/4 x 92 1/2 in.)

collection Mark and Nedra Oren, Coconut Grove, Florida

In the immediate aftermath of an inferno, smoke still rises in a phantom, almost architectural, cloud above an empty nursery that has been charred to cinders. Separating the tiny, undamaged beds in the foreground from the darkly silhouetted cribs behind is an obscuring wall of black smoke. This backward sequence suggests a regression from childhood to infancy, from defined recollections to the dimmest of early memories. Like abandoned watchposts, little chairs closely positioned by the cribs and beds indicate that mothers or other visitors have deserted the ward. The floor is reflective as if flooded with water, perhaps to douse the flames, and furniture floats on its glassy surface like boats on a placid sea. There is a dreamy subjectivity in the mirrored reflections, yet the screaming yellow background projects an unnerving anxiety.

From within the dense black smears and grey smudges of the Rorschach-like tableau emanate a deep melancholy and alienation. The sources of this malaise are to be found in the primary, most vulnerable, stages of life. The mind apprehending itself, its own history, discovers at its core the devastation of security, betrayal, an ineradicable terror hidden behind dark-ness. In the painting's foreground, a small, empty bed subtly draws one closer to rest, to be transported in dreams, while overhead the residue of destruction, of lost innocence, creates its own nebulous afterlife.

Louis Grachos

Nadie Olvida Nada, 1982
acrylic on hardboard
variable dimensions

collection of the artist
courtesy Sperone Westwater, New York

The series *Nadie olvida nada* is a launching platform in the production of Guillermo Kuitca. It is about the work of an artist that in 1982 still was not– or was only in part– what it would be years later, but that contained an immense burden of future. That burden that at the same time acts retrospectively on the image: with today's eyes, looking back, as sign of what would come.

Nadie olvida nada functions as an entrance door to Guillermo's work. From the title there is a poetic and pictorial incitation, but also historical to the memory of the spectator. So in this sense it is about a series that could be questioned by sight in the search of the embryonic elements that generated good portion of the later work. Like any key point in an artistic development, it also constitutes a paradox, because it opens a phase and at the same time closes another. But to what point is it possible to question a work for its derivations, for all those future images from which it is the antecedent but not the cause?

The series contains an ethereal and multiple space, in which the figures and the objects are displaced. But there is also, for the first time, a sign of organization for the space in scale, that remits everything to a beginning, to a structure, where the spatial continuum is traced by the objects that are disposed in their coordinates. It also stars to establish a repertoire of strongly symbolic images: woman, bed, chair. Interior space is born, enclosed and polyfunctional with regard to his previous work. Born also is the theatricality of the situations.

The works painted on wood function as a substitute to the blackboard, the place where they write the things we are not to forget. And the scholastic period is also in this series. Infancy is the privileged scenario to which memory recurs because that is where the footprints of the first apprenticeship are inscribed.

In 1982, before Kuitca obtained his profile as an international artist, his work produced in Argentina was to be shown, fundamentally, in his country. There was a different relation, of homogeneous context, between the place and the conditions of production and the immediate addressee of this images. That's why with the most elemental technics of pedagogy and didactics, the works of Kuitca recuperate– in that moment– a recent memory, that evokes with a divestment and a poetic precariousness, to the alone women or jealously guarded-torn,mutilated, or before empty beds or fenced by men, in situations where the limit is undrawn between protection and coercion — because of the political violence of the terrorists State and the War of the Malvinas. From the work, Kuitca evoked– and dramatized– a chain of tragedies caused by the dictatorship that was starting to end. The title of this series is premonitory and succedaneous of the *Nevermore*, the report elaborated by the democratic government about the criminal State that was built by the Argentine military.

These works begin to be associated to nucleus of senses that attached to them for ever. And that is the sign that *Nadie olvida nada* is been transformed in the image of a classic.

Fabián Lebenglik

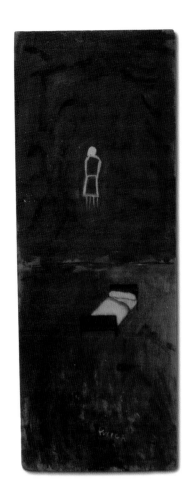

Mi Hijo Es Bello Como el Sol, 1982
acrylic on wood
42 x 191 cm. (16 1/2 x 75 1/4 in.)

collection of the artist
courtesy Sperone Westwater, New York

An obscure frond fills the extension of the painting and in it, two woman figures, that could be just one and her double, her brief displacement in the insatiable and fleeting course of a dream, where desire and the search for the lost is settled. There is, also, sheets carefully set in order, as if waiting for the son that is not there, which is the promise of a return always postponed.

The woman, that is not looking at the spectator, that is backwards, seems in fact to be searching in the middle of the foliage, blindly, like in old tales of fairies and children lost in the depth of the forest. And the bed is her bastion, the place of the first nurtures, the place of possession that is now as unprotected as she, as the mother, away from home, in the middle of the jungle. The bed is empty, it represents the absent, it is the expression of that emptiness and that absence, and is a hope, the intimate, uncontested illusion of rocking the son again, to shelter together under the blankets. That is why the bed accompanies this woman in her search, because it is the condensation of her power and desire.

Of course it is possible to imagine this tale in another way: to suspect, for example, that she is lady of fragile body that goes walking and finds all of a sudden a curtain where someone sceptically has painted a denseness and a bed and at the foot of the painting: *My son is beautiful as the sun.* And one observer of the painting, believes that such an affirmation should be in the middle of a very intense yellow. But the phrase is dropped, untediously written and very marked, very visible. as if it was drawn with a mixture of pain and affirmation of the happiness, because that is what resonates in the seven words that spell *Mi hijo es bello como el sol (My son is beautiful as the sun).*

Lelia Driben

Si Yo Fuera el Invierno Mismo, 1985
acrylic on canvas
125 x 195 cm. (49 1/2 x 76 3/12 in.)

collection Humberto Ugobono, San Juan, Puerto Rico

Having been raised within a paternalistic family nucleus where the figure at the cusp was a psychoanalyst, I always had the sensation that between reality and the unconcious there was no great difference. I remember the visits of my uncle, who used to stay at our house and install himself in my bedroom for days on end. By day we would ingest the obligatory psychological soup, and by night my uncle would recreate all that went on just over my head, in my father's office. Through these doors passed personages who, in spite of their apparent futility, were to my eyes encircled by an aura very close to that which surrounded Duchamp in the chess-playing days of his supposed retirement. I acted like a sort of paparazzo sans camera, spying on their comings and goings from the second floor of the house.

My uncle, who in a psychiatrist's diagnosis would be labeled as a schizophrenic, held conversations with (as far as I could count) at least seven different persons. They were always difficult to decipher, but one of the personages was an astronaut and another, I am almost certain, was a soldier from the American army (in spite of the authentic Caracas accent) in the thick of the Vietnam war. Many times I listened to the blasting of the bombs, I saw how the bodies of the enemies flew into a thousand pieces; and I was never afraid. The almost complete transparency of my uncle's escapist ravings, his distrustful but irresistable position concerning the boundary between good and bad, seduced me to the point of comforting me. At least this was so, as far as his deliria (lets call them dreams) went, even if at the beginning the adaptation to murmurs which unfolded into multiple voices, and which issued every night from some corner of my bedroom, really made me rethink the terms of mental equilibrium which guided my family's behavior, especially considering the fact that it wasn't I, a child of less than ten years, who had decided to sleep in the same room as my uncle; much less had it entered into my head to invite him for this purpose, in spite of the many times that he had compensated perfectly for the absence of playmates.

If I could recreate this scenario, this sort of speaking womb into which my bedroom was converted, afor some years, by my uncle's fantasies, I think that the only place to situate it would be that space in which discrepancies are almost as real as the unconcious: painting. This is definitely the place in which I would sit and remember that confusion between deliria and dreams by which my uncle introduced me to the world of art.

Jesús Fuenmayor

Siete Ultimas Canciones, 1986
acrylic on canvas
131 x 201.9 cm. (51 1/2 x 79 1/2 in.)

courtesy Bacardi Art Foundation

The painting pictured here, *Siete Ultimas Canciones*, from 1986, is a classical Kuitca-esque, atavistic mystery-play, in which pictorial clues suggest points on a kind of psychic map. it exists within a representational half-state, at once clearly delineated and spatially nonsensical. Along with many of Kuitca's painting from this period, for example, it evokes a darkly theatrical bedroom interior, yet a ghostly moonrise appears indoors here against checked wallpaper, and a Narcissus-figure is reflected in what appears to be a bedside pond. Insidious and obscure, fraught but not quite nightmarish, the painting conjures up the fantasies of a wakeful child — an *early modern* child, perhaps. Its fevered atmosphere, conveyed by furtive little pictorial incidents and skittish brushwork, remind me of avant-garde painting in Vienna before World War I — the emotionally exacerbated mood of Schiele's anorectic youths, of Kokoschka's degenerating physiognomies. But unlike these avatars, Kuitca's neurotic bedroom drama does not seem to be focussed on a particular subject or perspective, whether directly observed or projected from within. Rather, it proposes something more along the lines of a detective reenactment, in which apparently unconnected places and events are somehow linked. For all its febrile foment, it has something of the actuarial intent of a diagram or map.

Within a year after finishing *Siete Ultimas Canciones*, Kuitca had of course such intentions and was putting charts and diagrams directly into his paintings – in *House with AIDS*, for instance, in which an actual floorplan figures over a bedroom wall, or in *Piano de Madrid*, wherein, conversely, small images of a bed and chair cast their intimate shadows onto a street map of the Spanish capital. By the early 1990s, he was simply painting maps on mattresses: Kuitca's metaphor had come full circle, yet his mystery remained intact.

Indeed, the more resolute contemporaneity of the artist's later use of readymade objects may have had an unplanned, digressionary effect. By incorporating what many viewers instantly perceive as Beuysian and Duchampian tropes, Kuitca in a sense put himself on the map - the reassuring historical context of unbroken formal and ideational routes - but may have inadvertently put some sleuths off his metaphoric trail. The traditional, two-dimensional format, repressed emotionalism and talismanic inscrutability of his most recent work in fact suggests a return to the poetic, and ineffably Viennese, source of early paintings like this one. I have never travelled to Kuitca's city, Buenos Aires, but I always think of it as the new Vienna, and in *Siete Ultimas Canciones*, I feel the ghost of 1912 and the spirit of the Freudian diaspora.

Lisa Liebmann

La Busca de la Felicidad, 1985
acrylic on canvas
118 x 193 cm. (46 1/2 x 75 3/4 in.)

collection of the artist
courtesy Sperone Westwater, New York

One **ne afternoon** I went to Guillermo's studio to see the painting. I helped him turn it and set it against the wall. Almost before seeing it I started with the questions.

There wasn't a lot. Guillermo had painted it in his studio at Gangallo Street in 1984 for an exhibition in Belgium. The painting went to Brussels rolled with other works but never left the gallery's back room. It wasn't even stretched. When the exhibition was over they sent the roll to the Argentine Consulate in Madrid, where Julia Lublin picked it up. Julia took it to New York and later to Argentina. It remained for four years at Marcelo T. de Alvear's gallery at 600 and later ended up at the depot on Malpu Street. In 1992 the painting went to trial together with other works that Julia Lublin refused to return. Some time later it was sequestered by Guillermo's lawyers. They locked it up in the studio's bathroom until Guillermo and Julia reached an agreement. Then the painting returned to the hands of Guillermo, taking it to his new studio at Virrey del Pino Street.

I finished with the questions and Guillermo went upstairs. I stayed alone with the painting for about twenty minutes.

Two months later I have Guillermo's book from 1988 open. On the right page the red from *Idea de una pasion* stands out. On the left a black and white reproduction of *La busca de la felicidad.* For however I try I can not remember the colors. The black and white transforms the painting into a drawing. The fact that it is a reproduction transforms the drawing into something that resembles a scenographic sketch. A sketch is always something previous, but in this case the man in the middle of the puddle, the naked body, the knocked down chairs and the untouched bed leave not doubt: the representation already took place. The decor of the scene is an artist's studio. The stretchers leaning against the wall surely hide other scenographies .

La busca de la felicidad didn't participate in any show or public exhibition and still has not been reproduced in color. The twenty minutes I spent alone with the painting must have been the longest time that any spectator had to look at it.

Martin Rejtman

Yo, Como el Angel, 1985
acrylic and oil on canvas
189 x 320 cm. (24 1/2 x 126 in.)

collection Jorge and Marion Helft, Buenos Aires

This is how things are encountered by he who arrives later. After-Art. Everything is as it was left by the events, there is no more than that heritage: the legacy of facts. What do they have in common the tumbled chairs, the fallen body, the beam of light that keeps illuminating the painted flesh of the angel, the petals poured over the floor, already dry or ready to rot ? They are intact. An odd prohibition to touch, like a curfew,bares over the painting, over the crime scene. As if an invisible hand had sealed where the facts took place and every sequel had the judicial value of an evidence or proof. What happened?, wonders he who arrives later, dragging his delay as a hangover, a headache, certain odors that the night before left on his clothes. It is not that the event matters. Not even precise that an event happened. It is enough with any of its doubles: a representation, a ritual, a farce. What happened (that lost tale) is not more than the result of an imperceptible and tragic difference: the after of theone who arrives later, the obstinate tardiness of the slow. Could he have said something if agreed on been present, while things werehappening, with the others.

He arrived after: too late to tell. Now he vigils the tale as one who vigils the dead. But his art, somber and mournful as it is, makes visible the world's intact condition, that fragile miracle that is only witnessed by the ones who always go slowly, each time slower, almost until becoming still.

Alan Pauls

Si Yo Fuera el Invierno Mismo, 1986
acrylic on canvas
137 x 190 cm. (54 x 74 3/4 in.)

collection Jorge and Marion Helft, Buenos Aires

Guillermo Kuitca's paintings often speak first to the child in me. I love entering them the way I used to enter illustrations of fairy tales, with a sense of wonder and curiosity, yet also with a certainty that what I was looking at was real. Real in a way adults never seemed able to understand.

This is the way I approached the painting *Were I Winter Itself.* Set in a deep, dark fairytalish forest of tall, brooding trees and mysterious light, it centers on a figure, sketchily defined in white, laying diagonally on the forest floor. Looking down on the body is a young man whose shoulders are hunched in tension and pain, but not, at least yet, in full despair. Between the two figures is a touch of red pigment suggesting injury or death, but not necessarily confirming violence. The impulse to begin piecing together a story is simultaneous with the realization that behind the figures the forest floor turns into a blue man-made floor. It ends at a fireplace surrounded with a patterned wall of squares monogrammed with the artist's initial K. In the foreground the grey and larger initial K completes the idea that this is Kuitca's canvas/stage set: it contains one of his familiar beds, only partially shown, and several of his chairs, one of which looks scorched. Suddenly one realizes there is no story here. That one must abandon the pleasures of imagination and the childish delight in fairy tales. Nothing is happening and nothing ever will happen. Kuitca is expressing a basic human truth and it is for the adult mind, not the child's, to gasp at the depth of the aloneness he conveys in this powerful picture.

Anne Horton

L'Enfance du Christ, 1990
acrylic on canvas
203 x 230 cm. (80 x 126 in.)

collection Aurelio Lopéz-Rocha, Mexico

In a letter of 1856 to a friend, Hector Berlioz qualified his satisfaction with a Paris performance of his oratorio *L'Enfance du Christ* by adding: "On a beaucoup pleuré..." Whether the audience wept in aesthetic or religious ecstasy was his correspondent's guess.

Something of Berlioz' ironic ambiguity– the spiritual ambitions of a noted non-believer– permeates much of Kuitca's work as well. And, like Berlioz, Kuitca's iconography is only teasingly Catholic when it does refer to the faith. He hints just enough to lead us into the dark corner of exegetic doubt. Whether we anticipate revelation or expect parody, we are lured toward a dead end and delivered to the artist, who greets us with the gentle, indulgent smile of humanism.

In this painting Kuitca recasts the tale of the Christ child as a family drama in a set of identical tenements. An architectural trinity of floor plans floats upward in isometric elevation within a barbed and incomplete hortus conclusus (The enclosed garden typically stands for the virgin birth) described by thorns. This angle conveniently emphasizes the floor's expanse of lumber to evoke a childhood spent in carpentry and foretell of a mystical life sacrificed to a wooden cross. A few bright stars twinkle forebodingly among the random marks and stains of a fictional space.

What gripping tragedy was foreshadowed in those apartments? Was Jesus born in this monastic Lager upon a bare mattress too small for coupling? After facing the corner of an empty room, did he overturn the seat of his paternal humiliation when his punishment was up? And who sat on this spotlit chair in the middle of the apartment and under whose interrogation? More chairs, toppled lamps, charred beds: new props for apocryphal Christian intrigues. Yet, with no visible access or egress, Kuitca sets his penal theater for a drama so private that the actors, like the audience, must remain hypothetical.

As other works by Kuitca testify, few of these elements were contrived for this one picture. The economy of his poetics, his reliance upon a small repertoire of symbols bearing ambiguous interpretations– basic furnishings, simple props, plans, maps– astonishes when so successfully deployed to accommodate a familiar narrative. Like the myths of Christianity repeated ad infinitum, Kuitca recycles his equivocal iconography with the faith that it will continue to generate meaning.

Marc Mayer

Planta Con Texto, 1989
acrylic and oil on canvas
200 x 140 cm. (78 3/4 x 55 1/4 in.)

collection of the artist
courtesy Sperone Westwater, New York

I n **Guillermo Kuitca's** finely articulated itinerary of symbolic forms the floor plan emerges as the embodiment of many of the concepts that he has been elaborating throughout his career. Distillations of his early images of rooms, the plantas, done in the late '80s and early '90s represent an intimate shorthand or code expressing the range of private emotions inherent in his art — from isolation, estrangement and fear to a desire for intimate enclosure and warmth. Floor plans, inextricably related to Kuitca's maps of both known and imaginary places, indicate the loci of the most private and confidential human activities, the places in which fantasies, fetishistic behavior or the simple mundane aspect of existence may be carried on without intrusion… or so we hope.

In this painting Kuitca has investigated collective human intimacies on several planes. The spaces he creates are carefully delineated. They are also exposed in an almost voyeuristic way; we see directly into these rooms from above. It is like looking into the rooms in a doll's house, knowing that we can manipulate the inhabitants or their possessions with a movement of our hand.

Each room is ringed by thorns. Kuitca has often expressed his interest in coopting the symbols of Christianity. In a number of his paintings, crowns of thorns or intertwined thorn branches may be read, at least superficially, as suggesting one of the instruments of Christ's passion. In *Planta Con Texto* these thorns might be equally understood as references to the constraints of Latin American Catholicism. More plausibly, though, we may comprehend them as cues suggesting those private obsessions, both sorrowful and ecstatic, that are common to each of us. Of course, this confidential passion is rendered mundane when described in any visual or verbal form. Nonetheless, the commonplace nature of personal fixation often forms the crux of collective emotion.

The text written across the surface of this painting enhances the artist's elevation of the ordinary and his fascination with the banality of obsession. The passage reads, in translation: "The person I'm thinking about is my only hope, after all defeats; he's separated from me by a wall, and he sleeps. The day after tomorrow he will mount a horse. They will call him king. Come my son. I'm going to sleep. They will call you with my name. I'm going to sleep. I want to see you on horseback in my dreams." Kuitca has said "these sentences are from a novel that I came across by chance. I consider it an anonymous text." This highly romanticized, incongruous, enigmatic and, in fact, fatuous melodramatic quotation has the same impact as the emotionally charged, but highly improbable situations in the tele-novelas (soap operas) made in Mexico, Argentina, Brazil or Venezuela that serve to define the quintessence of passion for millions of people throughout Latin America. The pleasure for Kuitca is in the serendipity of discovering this text which he then appropriates, using it to underscore the despair of the banal which radiates from this painting whose images project out from a raw canvas enhanced with stains of searing yellow.

Edward J. Sullivan

Esa persona en la que pienso, que es mi única esperanza después de todas las derrotas, está separada de mí por una pared y duerme. Pasado mañana montará a caballo. Lo llamarán rey. Ven hijito. Me duermo. Te llamarán con mi nombre. Voy a dormir. Quiero verte a caballo en sueños.

Untitled, 1992
oil on mattress
200 x 200 cm. (80 x 80 in.)

collection Patricia Phelps de Cisneros, Caracas

The Maps are Wrong, The Paintings are Right: Slices of life, pieces of the world. Dream maps to sleep on (made on mattresses). Highways become bloodlines, capillaries varicose across bumpy surfaces. Land becomes skin, Wilmington is a button, so is Lancaster and Harrisburg and Reading and Allentown and Baltimore: Babe Ruth is from Baltimore, American places with American names.

The maps are wrong, the paintings are right. I was a long distance truck driver from 1982 to 1985, so I know. I must have driven from New York to Florida a hundred times. Kuitca moves stuff around. Where's interstate 95? Where's the Chesapeake Bay? I'm lost. That's good. Everyone loves maps. Not many people have figured out what to do with them. These maps aren't fiction, they're not fact, they're worlds.

Grids of modern life. Intricate, delicate and laid out with a fictive hand and a wanderer's touch: a scale much greater than 100 miles to the inch is whispered. Thousands of human beings and volumes of thought without depicting a single figure (not bad... its like flying), an overwhelming immensity by the simplest– the dumbest– of means. Finding the grid– that staple of modernist abstraction– in real life, Kuitca returns it to painting, infused with the sense of loss and hierarchy, anonymity and placeness that are a part of that life.

Afterthoughts: New Jersey lunar landscape, 11:30 PM, November, early '80s, 95 south, alone, tired already, radio playing. Romantic visions of on-the-road fading into $110 a day plus $25 for food. 199 miles to Baltimore, another 45 to D.C., 600 miles from New York to the North Carolina-South Carolina border (not even halfway to Miami). A Days Inn in Lumberton, N.C. where a whore asked me for "a date". Baltimore behind me. Lost in the night, staring at the map: all the places I'll never go to because I'm wrong and the map is right... shit.

Jerry Saltz

Nordrhein, 1992
oil on matttress
198 x 198 cm. (79 x 79 in.)

collection PaineWebber Group Inc., New York

Kuitca's *Nordrhein* (**1992**) presents an apparently accurate image of a road map of the northern German state of North Rhine-Westphalia. Essentially monochromatic with black on dull yellow ground, the painting is meticulously executed on the smooth, slightly undulating Naugahyde covering of a large square mattress. Kuitca plays up the idea of maintaining his mattress as a mattress by punctuating the surface with buttons at the locations of major population (and art?) centers (Köln, Dusseldorf, Essen, Wuppertal, etc.). *Nordrhein* is one of a supposedly ongoing series of works based on maps of cities and geographical regions (frequently altered or fictionalized), which Kuitca elaborates by varying formats, supports, and materials. For several of these paintings, beginning around 1989, he has made use of real beds or, as with *Nordrhein,* he has chosen to employ a readymade mattress alone and physically displaced it from its practical orientation to a vertical position on the wall.

Nordrhein extends Kuitca's exploration of the penetrating feelings that he has embraced and that we have learned to recognize more confidently in works created over the course of a decade and more — feelings associated with childhood memories, adult condition of alienation. His expressions of these feelings have depicted beds in airless interior spaces, they have taken form as regularized arrangements of actual painted beds, and they have utilized mattresses recurrently as arenas of intimate experiences from birthplace to bier. *Nordrhein* recalls many of Kuitca's previous references, while appearing to mark more specific concerns in his process of coming to terms with personal history and with more worldly aspirations.

To make art on or with beds would seem a heavily freighted activity for a painter to pursue after the presumably definitive example of Rauschenberg's *Red* of 1955. But Rauschenberg' notion to parody Abstract-Expressionist excess by means of paint-splashed bedclothes probably exists as inconspicuously as countless other modernist instincts within Kuitca's work overall. In his own paintings on beds and mattresses, Kuitca has projected a uniquely autobiographical terrain, as maps which chart his inner self. In *Nordrhein,* he has declared his art international perhaps more clearly than ever before.

Robert Rainwater

Untitled, 1991
mixed media on canvas
243 x 192 cm. (96 x 74 3/4 in.)

collection of the artist
courtesy Sperone Westwater, New York

From: floor plan to street plan;
  interior to exterior;
  country to continent;
south to north;
eye to brain;
real to ideal;
low to high;
one place to another;
clear to cloudy;
the known to the unknown;
pedestrian to aerialist;
left to right;
land to water;
color to tone;
tangible to ethereal;
man to bird;
caterpillar to moth;
native to tourist;
Icarus to Superman;
one perspective to the next;
earth to paper;
land to line;
intellect to emotion;
private to public.

From canvas to mattress.
From here to there.

Marvin Heiferman

Untitled, 1994
acrylic on canvas
199 x 189 cm. (78 1/2 x 74 1/2 in.)

collection Ron and Ann Pizzutti, Columbus, Ohio

The floor plan that has functioned in Kuitca's art as the boundary between self and world can no longer contain its fears and dreams. That ever present, protective two-bedroom apartment is now but a vestige, a symbolic reminder, little more than a shadow or scab in the sky. Beds of every variety that track the cycle from birth to death, and repeated views of the same straight-backed chair that suggests a witness or, more generally, the process of reflecting on one-self, are now scattered in what looks like a state of abandon-ment. Some are merely shadows reflected in a watery pool, others smolder, filling the sky with smoky flares. All this seems to say that the old order is no longer working, the fires suggestive of an attempt to burn off parts of oneself. But, as most belief structures teach, in destruction is creation, and the sensuous, fleshy tones that seem to vibrate up from the ground anticipate renewal on the horizon just as the two doors offer both a way in and a way out.

Allan Schwartzman

People on Fire, 1993
mixed media on canvas
193 x 280 cm. (76 x 110 in.)

collection North Carolina Museum of Art, Raleigh
purchased with funds from various donors by exchange

In **People on Fire,** Kuitca charts a bleak human terrain. Instead of towns, the road lines connect people, stitching a taut fabric of names, faceless others of our species. We read them as we might read stones in a cemetary, presuming significance in the rhythms and coincidences: *Laura Orellana, Ramon Rivas, Gabriela Rivas, Juan Pablo Villa, Helena Rivas, Joaquin Burgos, Monica Pratti, Norberto Podesta, Selva Orfila, Alfredo Rivas, Ariel Rivas* — ourselves by any other name. With the routine fervor of a clerk, the artist diagrams this community, ordering and systematizing, even color-coding each name by gender: male-orange, female-pink. Oddly, he leaves several sites blank, explaining them as symbolic of the people unknown yet connected to the whole. But to anyone aware of recent Argentine history, the blanks would as readily call to mind the *Desparecidos*, the thousands of the artist's countrymen who "disappeared" in the military terror of the late 1970s. Still, there is more than random fear and menace. There is something grandly apocalyptic in this image of the human tribe encircled by roiling washes of carmine and ash. Against the chaos, the intricate architecture of kinship and relations seems little more than a jerrybuilt folly. Here, in time for the millenium, is a prophetic vision of the burnt and the burning.

John W. Coffey

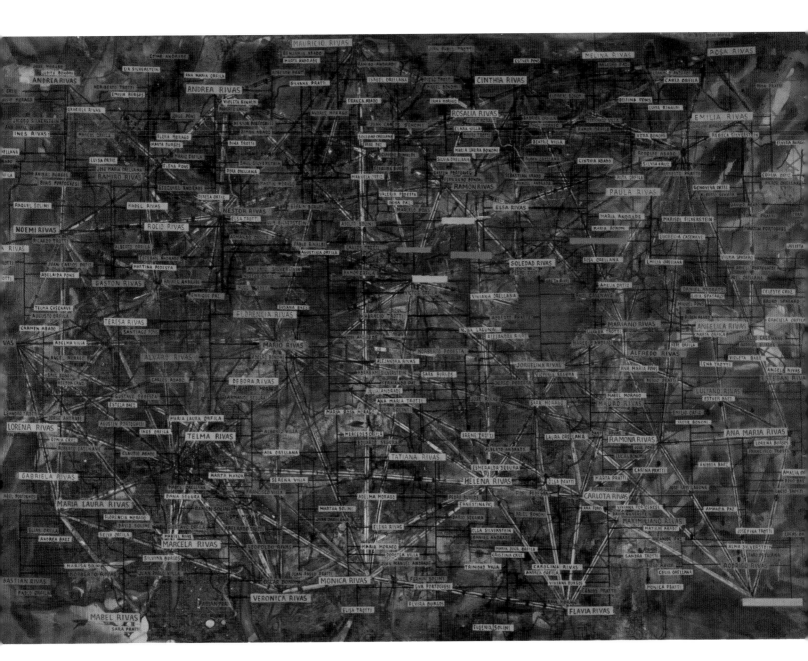

Untitled, 1993
mixed media on canvas
190 x 190 cm. (75 x 75 in.)

collection David Meitus, Chicago, Illinois

54

Douglas Blau

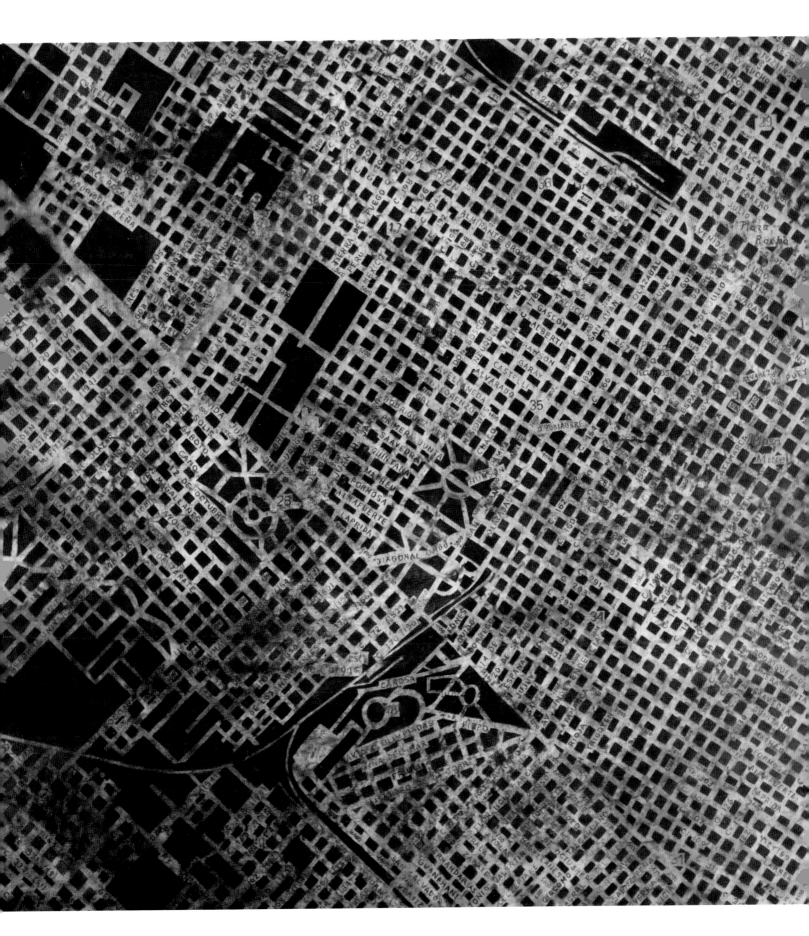

The Tablada Suite II, 1991
graphite and acrylic on canvas
190 x 160 cm. (75 x 63 in.)

collection Carlos and Rosa de la Cruz, Miami, Florida

(1)

Thought of teeth at first. Upper and lower hoof-shaped rows of teeth. Then the upturned toothy curves became skeleton smiles.

(2)

Powder blue is a color that implies the sanitary obsessions of the dentist's office, the doctor's office, or chlorinated water, which is, in fact, water that has been killed.

(3)

The powder blue is smudged with graphite as the artist drags his hand across it with a pencil in order to draw a seating plan of a concert hall.

(4)

There is something kind of obscene about smudged powder blue. It conjures up dirty children, dirty medical offices, dirty swimming pools; dirty things that are supposed to be clean.

(5)

I am left-handed. I do not write in pencil or fountain pen because I drag my hand across the paper and smudge it. In grade school the side of my hand was always black with graphite which I would try to clean off with spit. For that reason Tablada Suite II made me feel slightly embarrassed.

(6)

Prisons, stadiums, and concert halls are places where we are made to relinquish or choose to exchange individual experience for mass experience. They are places where we are not in control they are.

(7)

Powder blue is a color nobody has an opinion about. It is institutional, medical, and decorative. It is a color whose function is to please as many people as possible on a fairly banal level. It delivers neither the pleasure of intense beauty nor the experience of discord, which remind us that we are alive.

(8)

I have always thought that there was something sinister about being entertained. The music swells, you raise your head in a gesture of pleasure like a cat being scratched under its chin, you look around you and everyone's chin is raised, smiling the same skeleton grin.

Matthew Weinstein

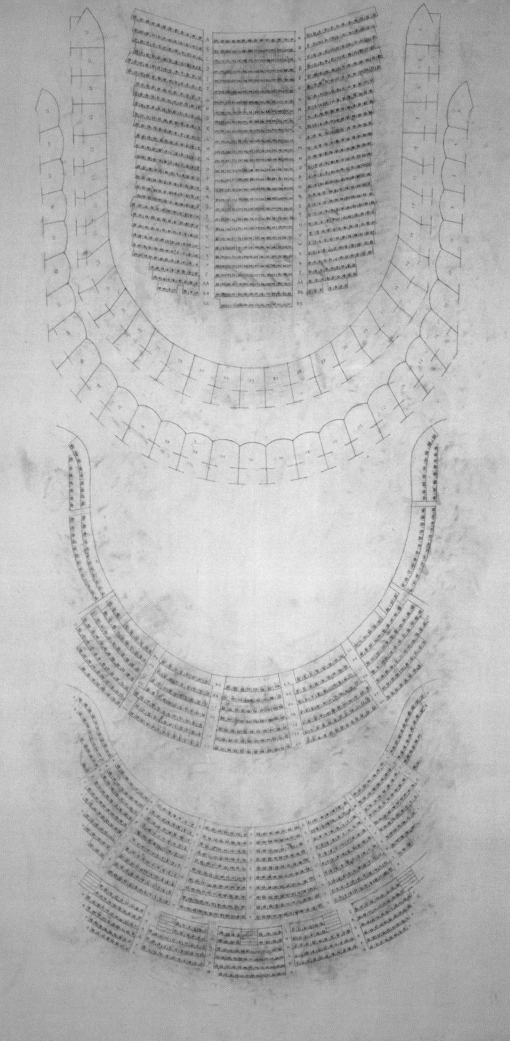

Untitled, 1991
acrylic on canvas
229 x 198 cm. (90 1/8 x 78 in.)

collection Carlos and Rosa de la Cruz, Miami, Florida

This painting is a network of tensions and contradictions. At first glance, there is an overall, abstract, diamond-shaped pencil grid with a series of rectilinear geometric forms subtly etched into its center. With prolonged viewing, the image reveals itself to be the mattress of a bed with an architectural floor plan recessed into it. Indeed the small living or working unit is hollowed so deeply into the bedding that its individual rooms are like tiny chambers with thick, tall walls. The painting's primary conflicts involve not only abstraction and representation, but also scale: How can an apartment be housed in a piece of furniture?

Then there is the question of flatness and depth: The top of a mattress is, of course, a relatively flat plane, while the dwelling is three-dimensional. That the architecture is rendered in extreme perspective emphasizes the contradiction. So does the surface activity of the canvas, which draws attention to the picture plane. The floor plan, drafted in pencil, evolves out of the line of the grid and is inseparable from it. In contrast, the paint is highly textured, imparting a sense of incident; it looks aged, stained, almost bruised.

Finally, there are the connotations of color. This painting is golden - not the conventional hue for a mattress. Bright yellow suggests sunshine and well-being, but also urine and mucous. The latter associations are underscored by the bruised quality of the surface. In contemporary cities worn mattresses, a component of the mobile dwellings of the homeless, often seem to bear the stains of bodily fluids. On one hand, the yellow used in this work evokes good cheer, on the other desolation, decay, and the notion of detritus.

Untitled, 1991, simultaneously speaks of abstraction and representation, macro- and micro-universes, hope and despair. Perhaps it actually resists titling, since there can be no summing up. Any hint of resolution would be antithetical to the nature of the work.

Lynn Zelevansky

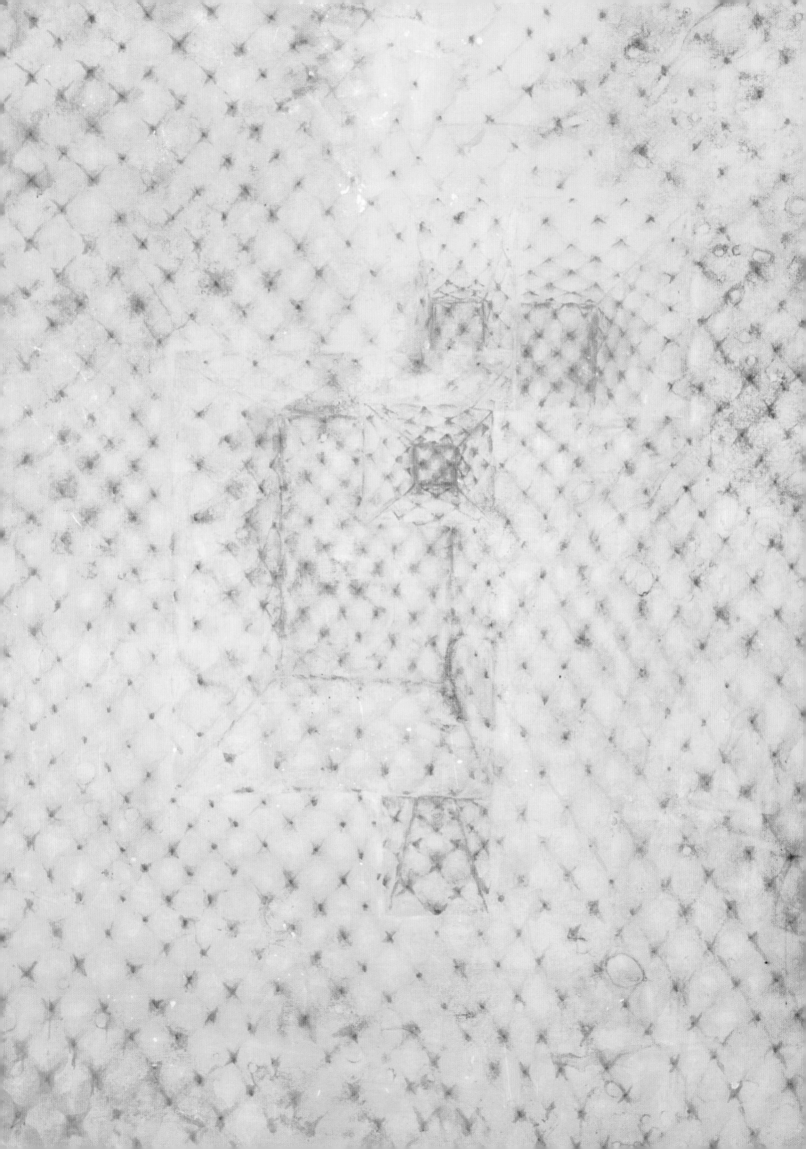

San Juan, 1991
acrylic on canvas
195 x 170 cm. (76 3/4 x 67 in.)

private collection

60

Echo (from the Greek ekho; sound). Repetition of a sound reflected by a solid body: certain echoes may repeat a syllable up to twenty times. That is precisely what happens with *San Juan*; its peculiar topography causes it to resound like an echo.

Miguel Miguel

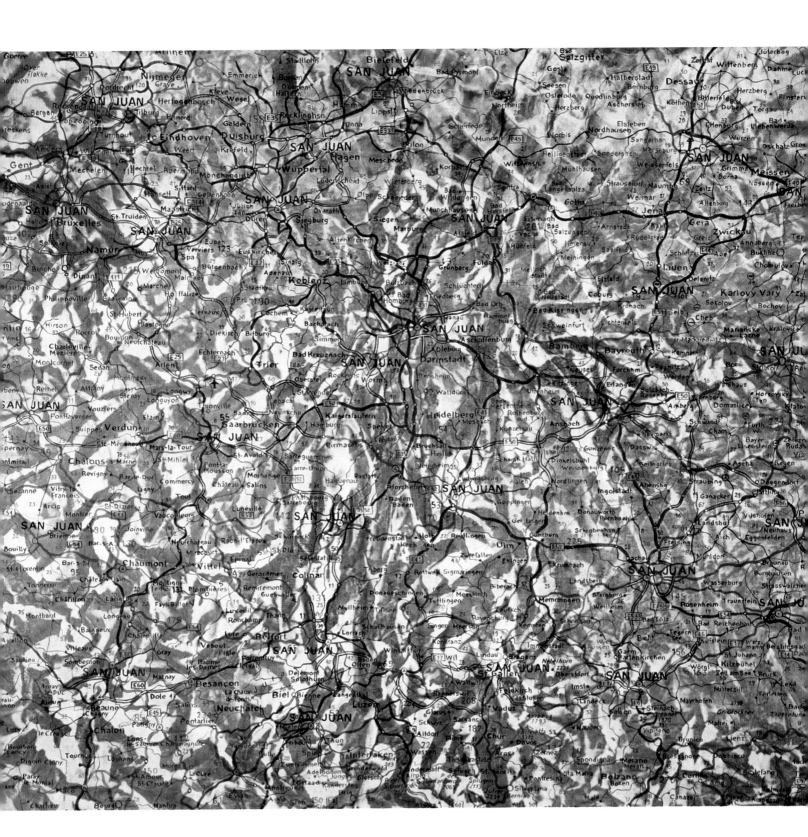

The Tablada Suite V, 1992
graphite and acrylic on canvas
181 x 126 cm. (71 1/4 x 49 1/2 in.)

private collection

62

Gravity-bound and ruled by geometries both plane and solid, architecture has for centuries helped painters to anchor their visions to Earth and to reason. What a shock, then, to see it in a strange new role, as a homeless phantom no more capable than a spiderweb of housing human beings. In Kuitca's architecture of memory, walls and roofs, ground and sky have all vanished, leaving only a free floating idea of a building that has come to haunt us from another era. Typically for the *Tablada Suite* (named for a Jewish cemetary in Buenos Aires, the artist's native city), this ground plan of a stadium belongs to a familiar utilitarian category we recognize as our own, but is magically transformed into a gossamer diagram that would evoke a time-traveler's archaeological reconstruction of a world similar to ours but as chillingly lifeless and airless as a distant planet. And the sheer size of this stadium (similar to, but not identical to Madison Square Garden) plunges us into awesome extremes of the gargantuan and Lillipution, shifting our scale abruptly from dimensions rivaling the French visionary architecture of the late eighteenth century to the miniscule rendering required to mark each of the myriad places for spectators. Incised with microscopic precision, this ghost of a building takes on further mystery as it becomes a fixed, abstract emblem that nevertheless hovers and flickers like an apparition. Suddenly, the static, centralized purity of these ovoid patterns that once teemed with noisy crowds looks as remote as a lost civilization, perhaps our own.

Robert Rosenblum

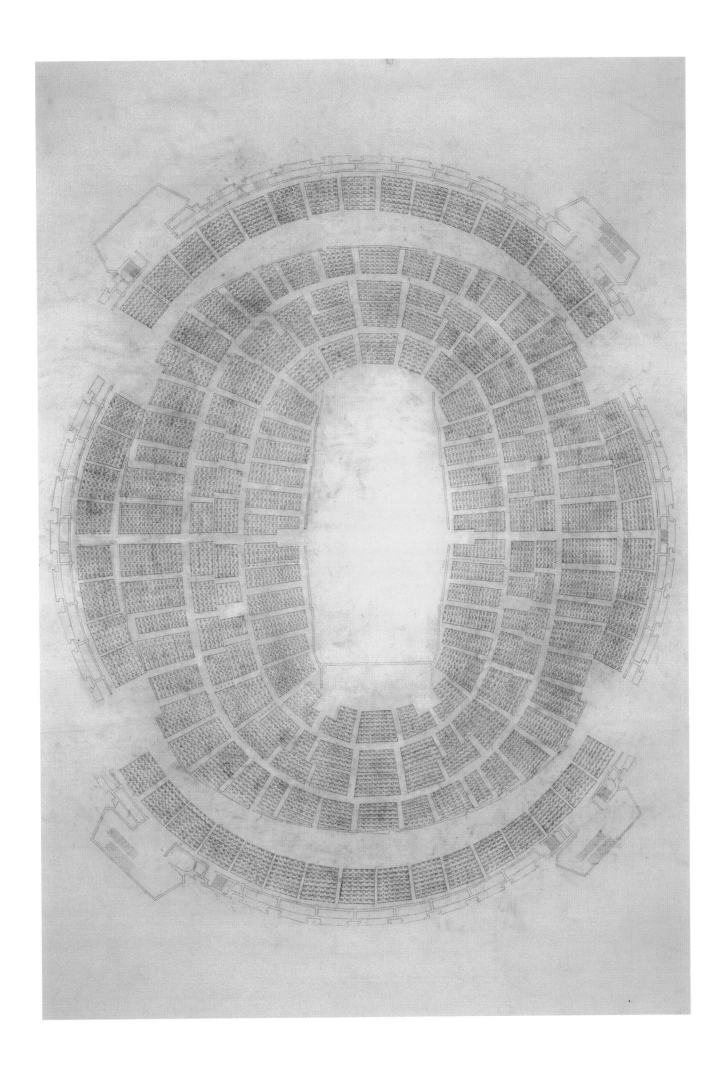

Untitled, 1991
acrylic on canvas
198 x 283 cm. (78 x 111 1/2 in.)

collection Moisés and Diana Berezdivin, San Juan, Puerto Rico

64

Dear Guillermo,

Placed before one of your paintings, I lose my sense of self, my sense of place. The familiar imagery, the exotic atmosphere of the scene confounds the pretense of equilibrium that I depend on to get me through the day. I feel lost and found all at the same time. The house plan, the vacant beds, the diminutive chair are given form by the careful yet passionate application of paint that draws me to the canvas' surface. I believe the scene is beckoning my participation in some wway; but am I ready to enter such a disquietingly empty place?

As I stare at *Untitled, 1991*, my mind suddenly ricochets to a passage from Susan Griffith's deeply provocative text *A Chorus of Stones: The Private Life of War.* I return to her writings periodically, especially when trying to grasp the complex interplay between private and public secrets, suffering and the role of creativity in coping with such overwhelming conditions. I quickly find the passage which I offer you here as a tribute to your artistic and spiritual genius:

> *The idea we have of reality as a fixed quantity is an illusion. Everything moves. And the process of knowing oneself is in constant motion too, because the self is always changing. Nowhere is this so evident as in the process of art which takes one at once into the self and into terra incognita, the land of the unknown. I am groping in the dark, the artist Kathe Kollwitz writes in her journal. Here, I imagine she is not so much uttering a cry of despair as making a simple statement. A sense of emptiness always precedes creation.*

Guillermo, thank you.

Sarah J. Rogers

Coming Home, 1992
acrylic on canvas
198 x 188 cm. (78 x 74 in.)

collection Josefina Ayerza, New York

There's a flickering gleam of violet light throughout the canvas, and this gleam, over a collision of shapes in the scribble of the words, stays subject to an uncertain floating space — at once plant, landing platform, *Home...* If lit-up specks, placed and traveling on straits, are also lines to be read, the floating space with worn-out elements and fathom rooms files over the *Coming* dilemma. Have words strolled to the heart of things?

At the tie of these figures and letters, it is the gloom of the sky toprescribe the direction that the eye must follow, or rather the dazzle of brilliance along which the look must shift the figures provisionally, a bit arbitrarily spread, here and there.

In the gloom of the sky... If the One that is unique picks up on the artist's Cinderella story with a whit of melancholia, as seen from *Home*, the dazzle of brilliance is instead the pure bliss– this painting followed Kuitca's first solo show in NYC– that divests him, in a One by One serial capture... close to every other lit up speck, in another place.

Not in fact a question of the letters taking the shape they designate, nor of the figures dissecting into linguistic elements, it is rather a question of intersection within the same realm. Which presupposes that figures and letters meet in still an other space than that of the painting.

Let's say that nostalgia is so powerful that it will take in the *Home* parts to quickly spread drama on the platform surface. Drama? Yes, in the figure of a foresaken microphone... in the cast of a fallen chair... in the silhouette of a tender wardrobe with a bowl of flowers on its far top... in the traits of a scarce kitchen... in the features of a classical bathroom... Why does the bathroom look like a face? Drama goes further inside the invisible head that is inside the invisible plane circling the skies in anticipation of imminent landing... inside your invisible head which is inside the invisible plane, *Coming...*

Coming? The one who is *Coming* is already gone; and this is why the artist did not paint the pondering head, nor himself inside the plane. He instead painted this very absence– of the artist, of the plane. Then this absence follows your own, mirrored in the stain that mimes your eyes looking out... from the holes in the bathroom?

The bathroom that looks like a face. If the key is in the recognition of this image, or rather in the recognition of the bathroom as an object that stands for the absent in the painting, the actual object in place of your disembodied look is inside the holes of this bathroom. A hole, a stain, it stands for your looking back at yourself from *Home* while *Coming...* while going, in the swing of a hammock that strives for indefinite projection...

Josefina Ayerza

everything is less, than it is, everything is more

Paul Celan

Untitled, 1992
mixed media on canvas
165 x 155 cm. (64 3/4 x 61 1/4 in.)

collection of the artist
courtesy Sperone Westwater, New York

In the movement of the hour, in the hour of movement what is it that we share, what is it that brings us together, inhabiting the same space. In what places can we imagine communities, spaces of communion, the exchange of tongues, the mingling of bodies, a gathering narrative of community.

It is these beginnings that I wish to speak. Fur such was the impulse that inspired the blueprints of early modernism, filling the workshops of artists and writers, composers and architects with dreams of communion, of a different order of community. Yet for those who come from afar, from the margins of the centre, the peripheral spaces, there can be no imagining the ideal body modernism promised, no idyllic state in which the self incorporated the other as himself, but rather always the nonidentity to self.

When Kuitca painted his *Tablada Suite* (1991-93), it was as if the thread of desires and fears with which cities are made (as Calvino writes) had become reliquaries of a utopian future envisioned in another time and place. One following another, the *Tablada Suite* becomes an architecture of social spaces whose lines speak of a community in absence. No longer is there the comfort of other paintings Kuitca offered before; spaces to dream and desire, places of congregation and retreat.

Each image hovers over a bare ground as if suspended in time. They seem to fall between form and its dissolution, a ground and its trace, both a material and immaterial space. The stadium and the prison, the theatre and the cemetery, the mausoleum and archive, each of them becoming abstractions, icons of an idea which remain nothing but traces. The thread which connects each to one another is a recognition that such blueprints can unravel, transforming visions of a future gathering into laborynthine structures of confinement and death.

Like Blanchot's "desoeuvrement", these paintings come to stand for the unworking of the work of art or literature, its lack of being neither present nor absent, the "retreat of what has never been treated." Brought together, they mark what the floor plan paintings had already presaged.

In the middle of the *Tablada Suite*, Kuitca painted another work that reveals in its kinship a secret itinerary into which we are being drawn. Based on a concert hall the painting, like the others, appears as both an abstraction and yet a mediation of its original desire. A place of gathering in which music mediates silence.

Writing of music, Roland Barthes spoke of how "the body passes into music without any relay", of how music is a field of signifying, not of signs. The uncanny power of music to take us out of ourselves, but by nothing more than something we can never recognize, reveals how frail, how insubstantial the body is, so readily overcome, too willing to be possessed. And yet what is given in the work of Kuitca is finally a form against which we might protect ourselves from the power of such an opening, such invocations of the body passing into music, of losing itself. Where we find ourselves is rather in a place where the dream of gathering remains, where representation faced with the disappearance of the body seeks to return to ground on which the self is rest assured.

Painting not only brings to us a sensual knowledge of the world as frail, but the longing for and fear of its limits, its finitude. It belongs to the world of the poetic, in the way that Celan will speak of poetry's tendency towards silence and of how:

Poetry maintains its ground at its own margins,
on order to exist, it must summon and extract itself
from its state of no longer existing to one of its still
existing.

We are faced with a place to which we will never belong, places already inscribed, to which we must abandon ourselves. The promise of communion exposes us to this separation and the aporias of history. This is the repressed archaeology of the city, the inhospitable spaces whose excavation reveals that it is we who are inhabited. And so to paint blueprints at this time is, in the end, to fold back upon the invention of ourselves and our ghostly beginnings.

Charles Merewether

People on Fire, 1993
mixed media on canvas
196 x 298 cm. (77 1/4 x 117 1/4 in.)

collection of the artist
courtesy Sperone Westwater, New York

When I heard that Kuitca was using geneological charts in his paintings, I thought it seemed like a natural evolution from the maps and house plans. It was another way to imply the presence of people, as he had done by painting maps on mattresses, and I had a preconceived idea of what these paintings would look like, based on his other paintings. Then I saw *People on Fire*, and I was completely surprised — first by the aerial view of a stadium (I hadn't imagined the geneological chart superimposed on another structure), and also by how perfectly the chart fit into the contours of the stadium.

If I followed soccer, which I don't, I would probably have made a connection between the fact that Kuitca is from Buenos Aires and that Argentina is a country of soccer players. Instead, the stadium image immediately struck me as ominous, which I assumed had something to do with my slim knowledge of Juan Perón and of dictatorships in general. I thought of Duvalier– of the Haitians who were asked to watch as political prisoners were shot in the palace courtyard– of Nazi architecture, of bullfights, and of Christians being mauled by lions in the Colosseum. When I described the painting to a friend, he reminded me of the Chileans who were herded into soccer stadiums and killed under orders from Pinochet in 1973. But it's entirely possible that there is nothing morose about this painting — that perhaps Kuitca thinks of the stadium or soccer as a metaphor for Argentina and its place in the world, and that the names in the chart, which give the impression of being of American and/or English descent, are a metaphor for Argentina's largely immigrant population. This is the real strength of Kuitca's paintings — they seem specific to the Argentinian experience, yet they are timeless and worldly.

Edith Newhall

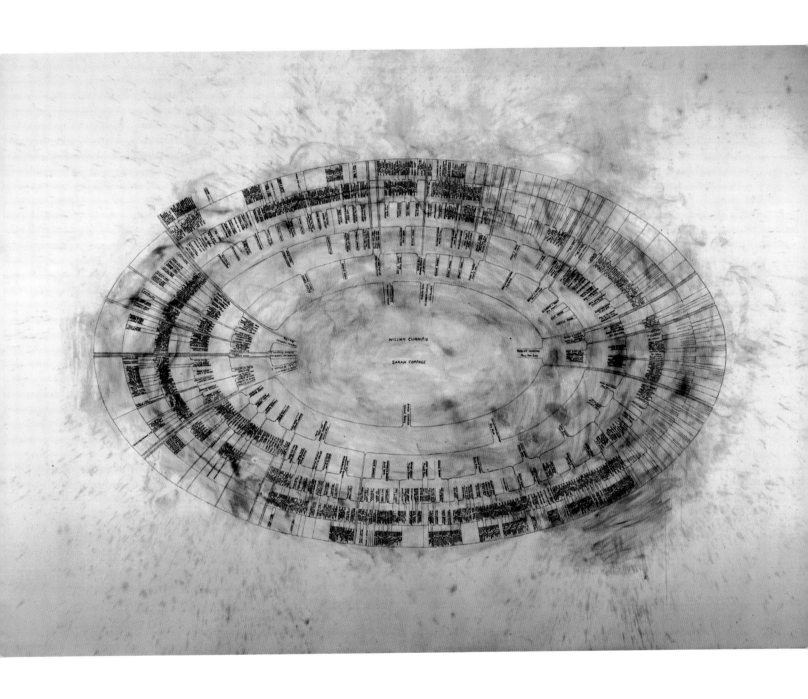

Coming, 1989
acrylic on canvas
237 x 237 cm. (93 1/4 x 93 1/4 in.)

collection Jorge and Marion Helft, Buenos Aires

72

The humidity of love resists in an empty bed, in a deserted bathroom,and in an unknown city, until displacing over the last frame of the tale. A spot over a chair, representations of keys and buildings, an apartment without tenants, the ground plan of a house turn into an intense light, routes that lead perhaps to Hamburg. A dining room with conventional furniture, a stage without actors, maps and neighborhoods with German names, rooms without familiar traces, a bed and a word: *Coming.* Kuitca fills each cell of the canvas– a succession of twelve throbbing and strange frames– with the limit of actions that could had been. A sole wink unites the parted tale:the stains of semen still warm. Desire wraps each image, trespasses each visual support to return over the same sensation of amorous encounter, of abandonment, of searching for the other. There is no history; there is no characters; there is no time; geography is distant in its conventional cartography and the house is artificial in its axiometric projection, in its ordinary presence. A sly and strange gray is lightly illuminated to let us (re)construct what could have been. The artist ties up every day realities without saying anything. But there is the game and the corporal friction Kuitca stresses in his discourse with few talking images; Kuitca sharpens his language with the austerity of whom murmurs a memory or suggests a dream or pushes a fantasy.

Coming is at the same time a work of closure that ties possibilities and shows answers and open questions. There is the furniture– emblems of his first series– the chair and the bed; there is the theatrical stage of his previous canvases; there are the maps and the apartments that dreamt their basic outlines of recent years; there are the words-signs with their literal habituality. The artist tangles up motives already worked in a display of twelve frames. *Coming* is an auto catalog, a concentration of ideas, some that are leaving and others that are adjusting, slowly, for the nineties.

> *... elixir del fuego central fuego justo fuego mango nocturno cubierto de abejas mi deseo un azar de tigres sorprendidos en los azufres pero el despertar estanoso se dora con los yacimientos infantiles y mi cuerpo de guijarro que come pescado que come palomas y suenos ...*

Marcelo E. Pacheco

Untitled, 1992
acrylic on canvas
282 x 373 cm. (111 x 146 3/4 in.)

collection of the artist
courtesy Sperone Westwater, New York

The city has been the locus of mankind's collective dream life since the beginning of urban habitation, and artists from earliest times have used the city as metaphor for the shared achievements and follies of humanity. Yet not since the metaphysical cityscapes of Giorgio de Chirico has a painter explored the imaginative boundaries of the modern metropolis with as much suggestive insight as Guillermo Kuitca displays in his map pictures. Among the most extraordinary of them is the large untitled canvas made in 1991 and exhibited at Documenta one year later.

Kuitca does not rely on massive scale to convey his potent imagery, and many of his pictures are conventionally sized. But the unusually large dimensions of this particular work are crucial in simulating a sense of engulfment akin to the urban experience itself and instrumental in stimulating the viewer's psychological response to this disturbing vision. Kuitca's frequent use of thorns, bones, and syringes to outline maps and plans in his paintings adds a terrifying symbolic aspect to schematic diagrams otherwise devoid of emotional content. Although he has discouraged political and social interpretations of his iconography, there can be no doubt that the syringes delimiting the streets in this map painting are an explicit reference not only to the rise of drug addiction in recent decades but also to the concomittant role hypodermic needles have played in the spread of AIDS. The artist's relentless repitition of the syringe motif, with one needle always leading to another all across the vast surface of this canvas, likewise evokes the endless nature of heroin dependency, here chillingly rationalized into an inescapable grid of a veritable city of hopelessness.

In *La Peinture Défi* of 1930, Louis Aragon wrote that "a juxtaposition of the early paintings of de Chirico would result in the creation of a town whose plan could be drawn." Conversely, this surreal town plan by Kuitca summons up real urban vistas all too uncomfortably like his bleak cartographic fantasy. Walking along the *Lungo-tevere de'Cenci* in Rome some fifteen years ago, one could see discarded syringes lying in the gutter in such quantity as to make this picture's imagery seem almost minimalist. And the open-air *Drogenmarkt* of present day Zürich is another demarcation of civic space for a solipsistic activity antithetical to the communal nature of city life. But direct enough is Kuitca's pointed choice of the syringe, an instrument that can make people shudder quite apart from extraneous references to urban dystopia. That directness is what gives Kuitca's art a unique sense of place within the disordered geography of the contemporary scene, in life as much as art.

Martin Filler

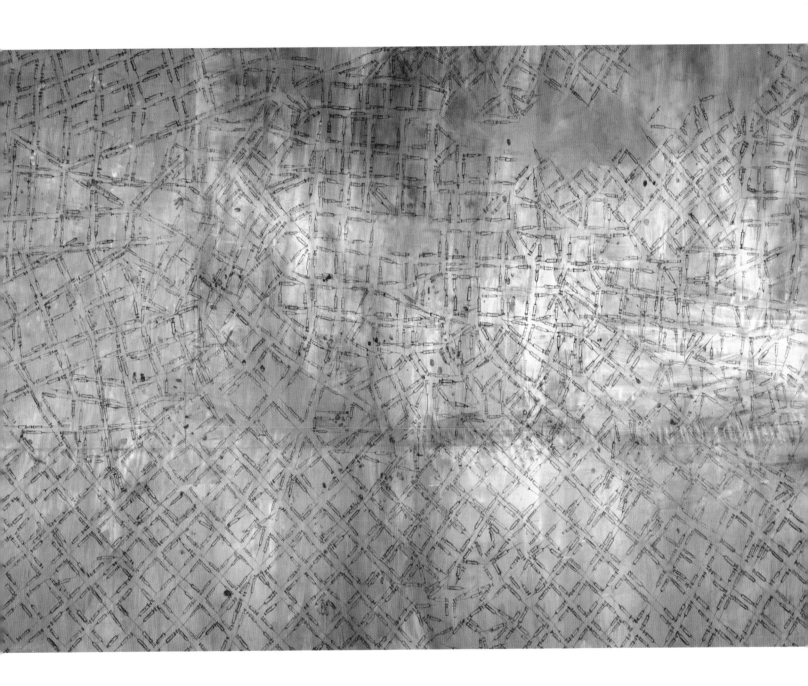

Corona de Espinas, 1993
oil on canvas
198 x 288 cm. (78 x 113 1/2 in.)

collection Ron and Ann Pizzutti, Columbus, Ohio

Negotiated Stalks: If you start from the center, which is black, and move toward the light, which is found in the brambles north, east, south, or west, you can estimate how you will feel, what you will feel, in the entanglements, and relativize the possibilities so you might choose beforehand what you want to feel and, indeed, how much you want to feel, so there is an idea you can control *life* — but you remember this is painting, so the final impression is of painted form in any one of the previously negotiated tubular stalks from space.

In the horror vacui of this untenable position, which crosses the starting point, one thanks God for the existence of black and white.

Richard Tuttle

Naked Tango (after Warhol), 1994
acrylic on canvas
195.5 x 148 cm. (76 7/8 x 58 3/8 in.)

collection of the artist
courtesy Sperone Westwater, New York

Footsteps of passion: The artist's paint-splashed feet glide across the canvas in sync with a Warhol beat. In this case, however, the step is Latin in its passion, the result a powerful floor plan of painted footprints. *Naked Tango* is as close as Kuitca gets to action painting– the debut of his feet as the brushes, his whole body as the pivot which directs the stroke.

Naked Tango is the product of an upbeat spark of intuition. In the framework of his oeuvre, the painting is but a brief sigh in a day's respiration. Tuning in on Warhol's classic dance step diagrams of the early '60s, Kuitca echoes an idea, updates a celebrated model with an inspired gesture. In his version, he injects the breath of life. A new dance comes to life with the vibrancy of the paint of these static tracks. The design is the message, the viewer's interpretation provides the content.

The tango is a topic close to Kuitca's core– a tribal dance of immigrants, intent on blending nostalgia for Europe lost with anxiety for America's tomorrow. These frozen footsteps are the painted proof of a cultural transition, the clues an anthropologist seeks to clock a society's change of direction.

This particular work has to do with steps, but not those of the tango we know; rather of the steps we need to take to discover new dimensions. He uses the Warhol layout to transform a known pattern into a new sequence.

Viewers discover an element that intrigues them in any work by Kuitca. His paintings propose new dimensions: a new "now" combined with the vision of a vaster future. He unveils that new dimension, inviting us to join him and occupy it, dance in it, paint in it . He takes something as simple as dance steps and spins them into a whirl of limitless potential. This painting proposes that we join him in the dance.

We must make the connection, because an unseen, unshared Kuitca is just a tattered road map in a drawer, a family tree without descendants, a silent dance studio bereft of rhythm. When the viewer joins the dance of *Naked Tango,* he sees, hears, even touches the tone of the tune just as a dancer does, just as Kuitca did when he gave birth to this moving snapshot of what appears to be a facet of a country's folklore, but in reality is a trip to a more universal dance hall.

Edward Shaw

El Mar Dulce, 1984
acrylic on paper and canvas
170 x 310 cm. (67 x 122 in.)

collection Sonia Becce, Buenos Aires, Argentina

1981 **Works on Paper** 1993

Works on Paper, 1981-1993
mixed media
variable dimensions

collection of the artist
courtesy Sperone Westwater, New York

Once, in a time of my life when I was drawing more or less constantly, in every situation, in restaurants, bars, subways, airplanes, hotel rooms, sometimes in my studio, always in bed, I one day realized that, having known Guillermo Kuitca for several years, I had never observed him drawing.

I was myself convinced that an almost obsessive practice of drawing was a necessary rehearsal for every line I put on canvas, and that this rehearsal could as well take place in public as in private. (Although these days nobody sees me drawing anymore) .

Today I realize with surprise that not only have I never caught Guillermo in the act of drawing, I have in fact until now never even seen a Kuitca drawing. Not having seen him draw, I became convinced he didn't draw. Yet here are these drawings.

The drawings here seem to refer only obliquely to the works on canvas; they seem to exist in a space between thought and practice. They are notational and persuasive, simple and fiercely emotional, comic and infused with melancholy. They look to me like drawings made in restaurants, bars, airplanes, hotel rooms.

The vocabulary of forms is commonplace: beds, coffee cups, apartment floor plans. The litany is more idiosyncratic: recitations of titles of popular songs, inventories of Saints, apparent arithmetic. The drawings indicate an exploration of both language and pictorial logic, they seem a product of either an almost drunken reverie or a precise methodology, or both.

Skeletal and emblematic, some of these drawings are barely pictures. They are notes from the artist to himself, a memory in process of formation.

Donald Baechler

Shit Disposal Houseplan, 1993

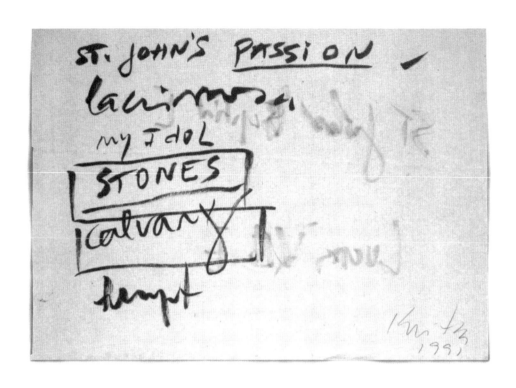

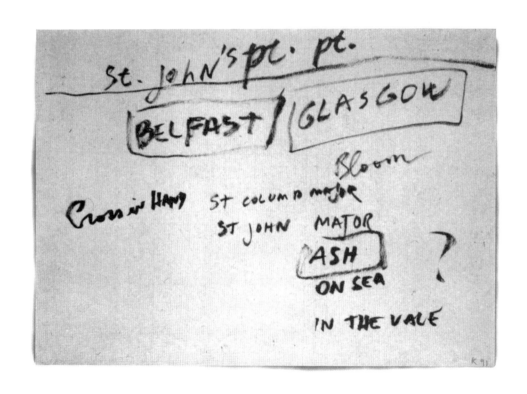

Adán y Evita, 1983

Untitled, 1984

Untitled, 1984

Ver, 1981

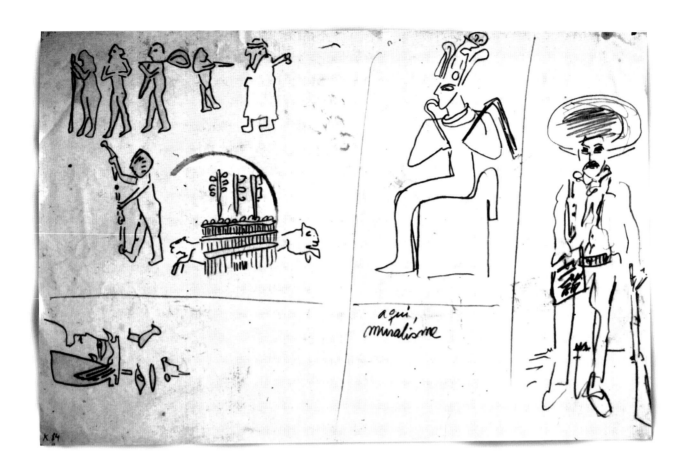

Suite Mexicana, 1984

Untitled, 1991

Untitled, 1984

Untitled, 1984

Untitled, 1983

Untitled, 1983

Untitled, 1983

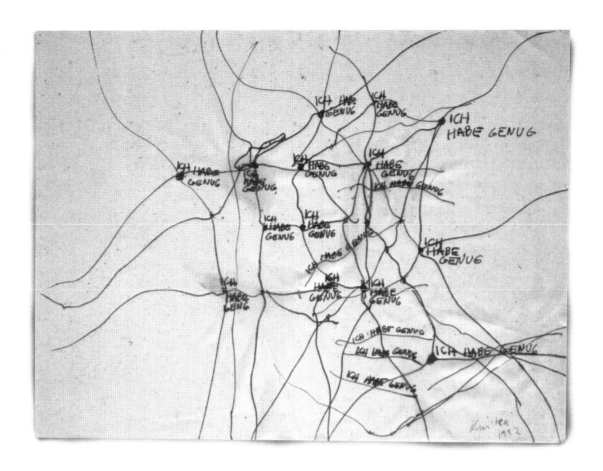

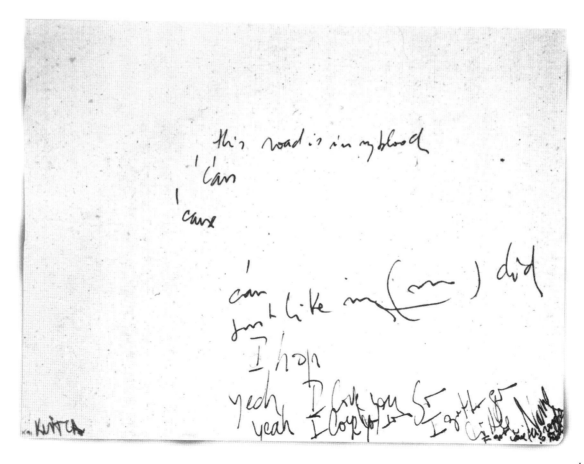

Ich Habe Genug, 1992

This Road is in My Blood, 1992

Nadie Olvida Nada, 1982

The Capitonee Houseplan, 1991

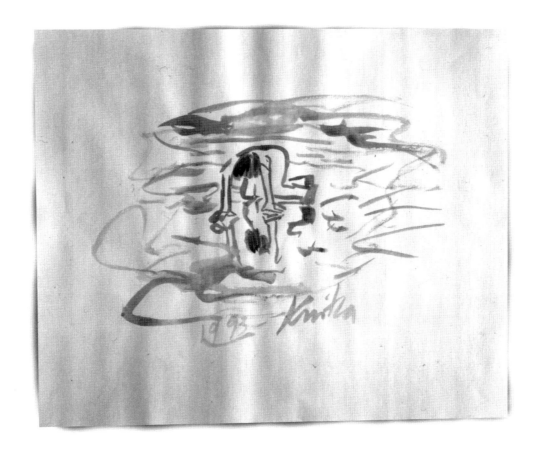

Untitled, 1993

Untitled, 1993

Untitled, 1981

Untitled, 1993
acrylic on mattress
installation IVAM Centre del Carme
Valencia, 1993
Collection of the artist

If a bed is usually a place of private reverie and personal comfort, Guillermo Kuitca's installation of myriad mini-beds completely subverts normal assumptions. Kuitca undermines the habitual solitude of sleep and somnambulance, but does not offer a sense of community in its place. The baby mattresses, scattered on the floor, are lonely and inhospitable. Instead of pillows, sheets, and other signs of snugness, Kuitca's beds are covered with maps. Depicting random cities in various countries, the maps do not unite the beds, but emphasize a sense of isolation.

The beds obliquely recall the children in Peter Pan . They would lay down in their little beds and then get carried off, far and away, to Never-Never land. Ideally, children's beds covered with maps would seem to be similar invitations for travel. In Kuitca's tableau, however, the map-strewn beds do not hold out the possibility for adventure. His maps eradicate national and regional distinctions - a map of Detroit looks incredibly like that of Poland. He eliminates the autonomy and distinction of each place. The maps are not allusions to exploration, but painterly standardizations of rational geography.

Maps represent the location of cities and towns; places filled with buildings, homes, people, and beds. Kuitca makes beds filled with cities. But everything is empty. No one seems to occupy these beds or these cities. Collectivity subjugates autonomy and isolation overrides association. His installation of potential poignancy drained of sentimentality is like an eerie chamber of childhood devoid of youthful juvenescence.

Alisa Tager

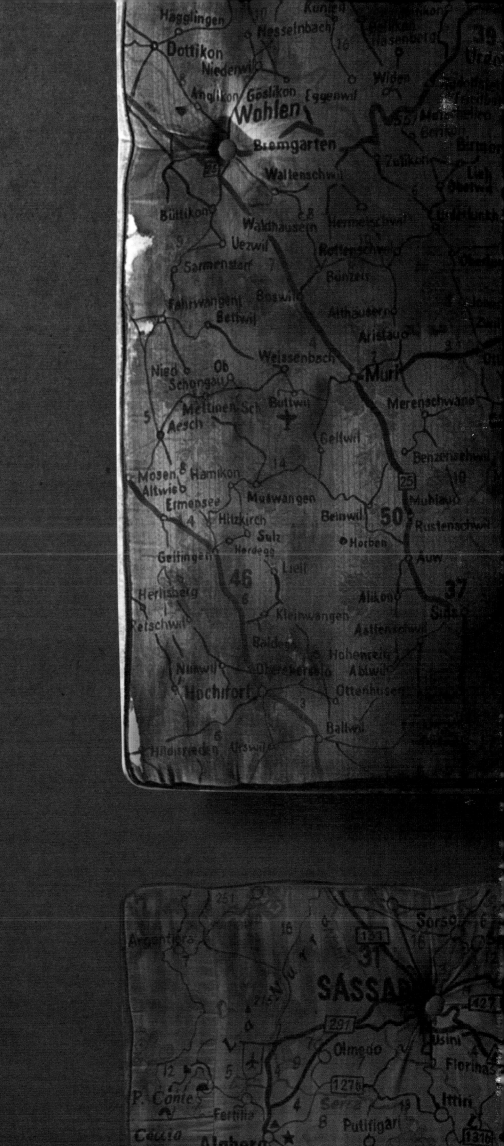

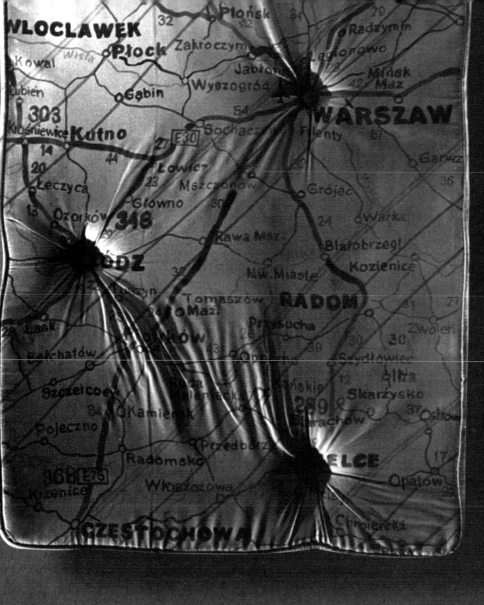
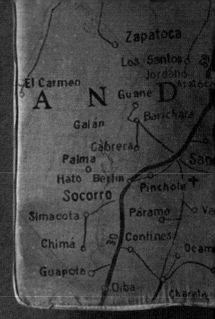
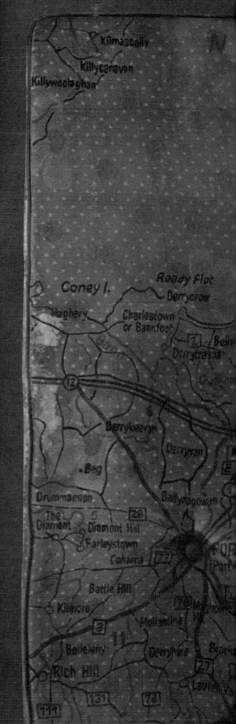

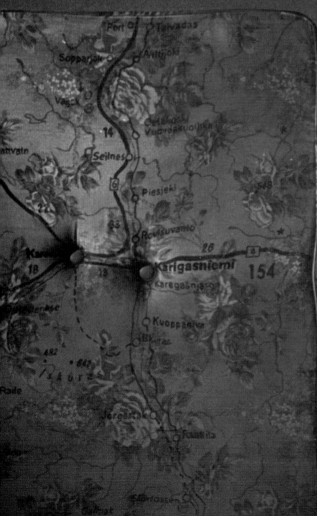

This exhibition of paintings, drawings and sculpture was made in Buenos Aires, Argentina, travelled through Miami, Florida on its way to Columbus, Ohio, and returned to the Center for the Fine Arts in Miami before travelling to London, England. Series of itinerant dislocations have become second nature to artists who have reached a high level of international renown, yet seem particularly appropriate to the work of Guillermo Kuitca. For Kuitca this late-twentieth century condition of global leap-frogging speaks to the core of his intensely private, yet strangely universal images. The runways of one city's airport become indistinguishable from another's, the veined skin-map of my country easily confuses with yours, one small home boxed into rectangles of private acts mirrors the neighbor's only inches away.

Where is home? Where are the boundaries drawn between personal and public space? Who is family? How do we chart the interior and exterior geographies of our lives? What remains when the curtain is lowered? The work of Guillermo Kuitca raises many questions as it addresses a journey of human obsession and whispered commonality – initially depressing, ultimately liberating. We are proud to give it a home in Miami, if only temporarily.

Kate Rawlinson
Center for the Fine Arts
Miami, Florida

S i yo fuera el invierno mismo ain't no ordinary lovers' quarrel. For one, it did not take place at home like most do, but on a stage, a stage with a vague landscape for a background. It has the symmetry of a good fight – two wooden chairs that, although far apart, are not on opposite corners like we would find in a boxing match. This ring, perversely, has only one corner. Two people, a man and a woman, in this century, albeit not exactly now. Sort of like Buenos Aires has been described to me, in this century but not exactly now.

More symmetry. A ghostly chair rendered useless by having been knocked down, its twin in the form of a spirit, also rendered useless by the passage of time in this century. We have to remember that spirituality, late in this century for us westerners comes in the form of crystals, Opium, Buddha, the Dalai Lama and other bits of orientarama.

The floor in this stage has been marked. I'm not convinced that they are the marks produced by a Tango. Having been born and raised in the Caribbean I possess more knowledge of Salsa, Son, and Meringue. I know the Tango from records and television. Never danced to it because I found it too soaked in theater. I prefer the lazy cadence of Boleros. Not Ravel's but Agustin Lara's.

Si yo fuera el invierno mismo, 1986
acrylic on canvas
110 x 252 cm. (55 1/2 x 99 1/4 in.)

Javier Benitez, Monterrey

This ain't no Tango. My memory tells me that in a proper Tango, the back of the female was always uncovered. Hers isn't. Carlos Gardel was called on occasion to lend his fabulous voice to other musical genres - Waltz, Pasodoble, Shimmy, and Rhumba. There is one of these anonymous songs, a fox trot in this case that I have always enjoyed, it is called *La Hija de Japonesita* (the daughter of little Japanese Woman) where a Geisha born of "traicion" pleads Buddha to save her soul before committing Harakiri. Sad.

Meyer Vaisman

Biography

1961 Born Buenos Aires, Argentina.
Lives and works in Buenos Aires.

Selected Solo Exhibitions

1974
Galeria Lirolay, Buenos Aires
1978
Galeria Christel K., Buenos Aires
1980
Fundacion San Telmo, Buenos Aires
1982
CYCA, Centro de Artes y Comunicacion, Buenos Aires
1984
Galeria Del Retiro, Buenos Aires
1985
Elizabeth Franck Gallery, Knokke-Le-Zoute, Belgium (catalogue)
1986
Galeria del Retiro, Buenos Aires (catalogue)
Thomas Cohn Arte Contemporanea, Rio de Janeiro
1987
Galeria del Retiro, ARCO, Feria Internacional de Arte
Contemporanea, Madrid (catalogue)
Galeria Paulo Figuerado, Sao Paolo
1989
Thomas Cohn Arte Contemporanea, Rio de Janeiro
Galeria Atma, San Jose, Costa Rica
1990
Gian Enzo Sperone, Rome (catalogue)
Thomas Solomon's Garage, Los Angeles
Stadtisches Museum, Mulheim
Witte de With Center for Contemporary Art, Rotterdam (catalogue)
Galerie Barbara Farber, Amsterdam (catalogue)
Kunsthalle Basel, Basel
Annina Nosei Gallery, New York
1991
Annina Nosei Gallery, New York (catalogue)
Galerie Barbara Farber, Amsterdam
1991-92
"Projects: Guillermo Kuitca," The Museum of Modern Art, New York (brochure); travelled thru 1992: Newport Harbor Art Museum, Newport Beach, California (catalogue); The Corcoran Gallery of Art, Washington, D.C.; Contemporary Arts Museum, Houston
1992
"Les Allumees Nantes-Buenos Aires," DRDC, Chapelle de l'Oratoire-Musee des Beaux Arts de Nantes, Nantes, France (handout)
Gian Enzo Sperone, Basel Art Fair
1993
"Guillermo Kuitca, Les Lieux de l'errance," Musee d'Art Contemporain de Montreal, Montreal, Quebec, Canada, 16 April - 6 June 1993 (handout)
Sperone Westwater, New York, 1 May - 5 June (catalogue)
1993-94
IVAM Centre del Carme en Valencia, Valencia, Spain, 26 February - 2 May 1993, and travels to: Museo de Monterrey, Monterrey, Mexico; Museo Rufino Tamayo-Instituto Nacional de Bellas Artes, Ciudad de Mexico, Mexico.
1994
"Guillermo Kuitca, The Tablada Suite," Sperone Westwater, New York, 30 April - 4 June (catalogue)
"Guillermo Kuitca: Obra Recente," Thomas Cohn Arte Contemporanea, Rio de Janeiro, (catalogue)
1994-95
"Burning Beds, Guillermo Kuitca: A Survey 1982 - 1994", Wexner Center for the Arts, Columbus, Ohio, October 1 - December 31, 1994, and travels to: Center for the Fine Arts, Miami, 29 January - 16 April 1995; Whitechapel Art Gallery, London, 5 May - 25 June 1995; Tel Aviv Museum of Art, Tel Aviv, Isreal, July - August 1995

Selected Group Exhibitions

1980
"Premio Braque," Museo de Arte Moderno, Buenos Aires
1981
"25 anos," Museo de Arte Moderno, Buenos Aires
1982
"La Nueva Imagen y "Pintura Fresca"," Galeria del Buen Ayre, Buenos Aires
"Gruppo IIIII," CAYC, Centro de Arte y Comunicacion, Buenos Aires (catalogue)
"La Anavanguardia," Estudio Giesso, Buenos Aires (catalogue)
"Bienal Arche," Museo Nacional de Bellas Artes, Buenos Aires
"Premio Braque," Museo Nacional de Bellas Artes, Buenos Aires
1983
"Intergrafik '83," Berlin (R.D.A.)
"Artes visuales y democracia, La Nueva Imagen de los '80s," CAYC, Centro de Artes y Comunicacion, Buenos Aires
"Realismo, Tres Vertientes," Museo de America, Madrid; Maison de l'Amerique Latine, Paris; Moscow and Belgrade
"Sieben Maler aus Buenos Aires," Centro Cultural Ciudad de Buenos Aires; Akademie der Kunst, Berlin; International Union of Architects, XV Congress, Cairo
"7 Pintores...," Museo Municipal Bellas Artes Juan B. Castagnino, Rosario, Argentina
"Expressiones '83," Museo de Arte Moderno, Centro Cultural Ciuda de Buenos Aires
1984
Centro Cultual Islas Malvinas, Buenos Aires
"Artistas en el papel," Centro Cultural Ciudad de Buenos Aires, Museo Municipal de Bellas Artes Juan B. Castagnino, Rosario, Argentina; Museo Provincial de Bellas Artes, Tucuman, Argentina
"Libros de Artistas," Centro Cultural Ciudad de Buenos Aires
1985
"XVIII Bienal," Sao Paulo, Brazil (catalogue)
"Ideas y imagenes de la Artgentina de hoy," Museo de Arte Moderno, Mexico City; Venezuela, Peru and Brazil (catalogue)
"Del Pop Art a la Nueva Imagen," Galeria Ruth Benzacar, Buenos Aires; Museo Nacional de Artes Plastica, Montevideo
"Instalaciones," Fundacion San Telmo, Buenos Aires
"Latinoamericanos en Nueva York," M13 Gallery, New York
"De la Nueva Figuracion y Nueva Imagen,"
Museo de Bellas Artes, Caracas
1987
"Arte Argentina 1810 - 1987," Istituto Italo-Latinoamericano, Rome (catalogue)
"Art of the Fantastic, Latin-America, 1920 - 1987," Indianapolis Museum of Art; The Queens Museum, New York; Center for the Fine Arts, Miami; Centro Cultural de Arte Contemporaneo, Mexico City (catalogue)
"La Nueva Imagen, Dos Generaciones," GAleria Forum, Lima
"Argentina, Pintura Joven," Galeria Arte Actual, Santiago de Chile
1988
"Salon Internacional Bienal," San Jose, Costa Rica (catalogue)
1989
"New Image Painting, Argentina in the Eighties," America Society Art Gallery, New York (catalogue)
"U-ABC," Stedelijk Museum, Amsterdam
Museum Calouste Gulbenkian, Lisbon
"XX Bienal," Sao Paulo (catalogue and individual brochure)
Thomas Cohn Arte Contemporanea, Kohn
1990
"Group Show, Paintings," Annina Nosei Gallery, New York
"Hommage to Van Gogh," Poster Design, The Netherlands, (catalogue)
1991
"Metropolis," Martin Gropius Bau, Berlin (catalogue)
"Personal Portraits," Annina Nosei Gallery, New York
"Landscape Paintings," Annina Nosei Gallery, New York
"Latin-American Artists," Arnold Herstand Gallery, New York
Rhode Island School of Design, Providence, RI
"Mito y Magia de los '80," Museo de Arte Contemporaneo, Monterrey.
1992
"Currents 1992: The Absent Body," Institute of Contemporary Art, Boston (catalogue)
Documenta, Kassel
"La Coleccion del IVAM," Instituto Valenciano de Arte Moderno, Valencia
"Greg Colson, Guillermo Kuitca, William Wegman," Sperone Westwater, New York

1992-93

"Group Exhibition," Galleria Galliani, Genova, Italy, December - January

"Latin American Artists of the Twentieth Century," Curated by Waldo Rasmussen, Estacion Plaza de Armas, Sevilla, Spain, 11 August - 12 October 1992; and travelled to: Musee National d'Art Moderne, Centre Georges Pompidou and Hotel des Arts, Foundation Nationale des Arts, Paris, 10 November 1992 - 11 January 1993; Kunsthalle Cologne, Cologne, 8 February - 25 April 1993; The Museum of Modern Art, New York, 2 June - 7 September 1993. (catalogue)

1993

"The Spirit of Drawing," Sperone Westwater, 121 Greene St., New York, 1 May - 12 June

Annina Nosei Gallery, New York, May - June

"Drawing the Line Against AIDS," Biennale di Venezia and AmFar International, Venice, June 8 - 13, curated by John Cheim, Diego Cortez, Carmen Gimenez, Klaus Kertess(catalogue)

"Group Exhibition," Galeria Namia Mondolfi, Venezuela, November

"Living With Art: The Collection of Ellyn & Saul Dennison," The Morris Museum, Morristown, NJ, October 16 - November 21 (catalogue)

1993-94

"Cartographies - 14 Artists from Latin America," The Winnipeg Art Gallery, Winnipeg, Manitoba, Canada, 19 March - 6 June, curated by Ivo Mesquita; and travels to: Venezuela, Colombia and New York.

1994

"Art on the Map," Chicago Cultural Center, Chicago, 30 April - 10 July

"La Ville," Musee National d'Art Moderne, Centre Georges Pompidou, Paris

"Mapping," Museum of Modern Art, New York, October 5 - December 20 (catalogue)

"Arrested Childhood", COCA, The Center of Contemporary Art, Miami, 19 May - 2 July

"Written/Spoken/Drawn in lacanian ink", Thread Waxing Space, New York, 3 May - 7 May

"La Metafora Trovata, 30 anni", Galleria Sperone, Rome, (catalogue)

"5 Artistas de las Americas," Sandra Azcarraga, Mexico City, 21 April - 27 May

Sperone Westwater, New York, Summer 1994.

"Prints from Solo," The College of Wooster Art Museum, Wooster, Ohio, 24 August - 9 October 1994.

"Argentina 1920 - 1994," The Museum of Modern Art, Oxford, 2 October - 31 December (catalogue)

Selected Bibliography

1982

Guillermo Kuitca, (Madrid: Galeria del Retiro, Centro de Artes y Ciencias, 1982) texts by Jorge Glusberg

1983

International Transavantgarde, (Milan: Gian Carlo Politi Editore, 1983) texts by Jorge Glusberg.

1985

XVIII Bienal Internacional de Arte, (Sao Paulo: Bienal Sao Paulo, 1985)

Restany, Pierre, "La Giovanne Generazione e il Desiderio di Vivere," Domus, (Milan), no. 661, May 1985. pp. 84 - 87.

1987

Art of the Fantastic, (Indianapolis: Indianapolis Museum of Art, 1987) texts by Rosa Brill, Holliday Day, Hollister Sturges.

1988

Cantor, Judy, "Kuitca the wunderkind painter turns 27," Buenos Aires Herald, 7 February

Gasteiger, A., "Kuitca," Juliet, (Italy) no. 38, October/November 1988. p. 23.

Guillermo in Rio, (New York: Ajax Press, 1988) Drawings and text by Donald Baechler.

1989

Guillermo David Kuitca: Obras 1982 - 1988, (Buenos Aires: Julia Lublin Ediciones, 1989) texts by Fabian Lebenglik.

Kuitca: XX Bienal Internacional Sao Paolo, (Sao Paolo: XX Bienal, 1989) text by Lelia Driben.

XX Bienal International de Arte, (Sao Paolo: Bienal Sao Paolo, 1989)

U-ABC, (Amsterdam: Stedelijk Museum, 1989) Introduction by Win Beren, "Turn the Map Upside Down," by Dorine Mignot, and "Three Decades of Art and Culture in Argentina," by Guillermo Whitelow.

New Image Painting, Argentina in the Eighties, (New York: Americas Society, 1989) texts by Louis Crachos and Jorge Glusberg.

1990

Bollo, Eric, "Guillermo Kuitca and Julio Galan," Metropolis Magazine, (Holland), No. 4, September/October, 1990.

Guillermo Kuitca, (Amsterdam: Galerie Barbara Farber, 1990) texts by Wim Beren and Edward Lucie Smith.

Borum, Jennifer P., "Guillermo Kuitca: Annina Nosei Gallery," Artforum, May 1990. p. 189.

Brenson, Michael, "Guillermo Kuitca," The New York Times, 9 February, 1990

Guillermo Kuitca, (Rotterdam: Witte de With Center for Contemporary Art, 1990) texts by Rina Carvajal and Chris Dercon.

Guillermo Kuitca, (Rome: Gian Enzo Sperone, 1990) text by Charles Merewether.

Homage to Vincent Van Gogh, (The Netherlands: Van Gogh Foundation, 1990) texts by Frits Beeht.

Feintuch, Robert, "Guillermo Kuitca at Annina Nosei," Art in America, September 1990. pp. 198 - 199.

Mahoney, Robert, "New York in Review," Arts Magazine, May 1990. p. 109.

Morsiani, Paola, "Interview with Guillermo Kuitca," Juliet, (Italy), No. 48, June 1990.

Pellizzi, Francesco, Julio Galan, (Rotterdam: Witte de With Center for Contemporary Art, 1990)

Shaw, Edward, "The End of Solitude: Young Artists on the Rise," Artnews, October 1990. pp. 138 - 143.

Smith, Roberta, "Guillermo Kuitca," The New York Times, 12 April

Van Nieuwenhuyzen, Martijn, "Guillermo Kuitca, Julio Galan: Private Apartments, Spanish Pain," FlashArt, November/December 1990. p. 149.

Ayerza, Josefina, "Guillermo Kuitca at MoMA," FlashArt, November 1991. p. 129 - 130.

Ayerza, Josefina, "Conversation with Guillermo Kuitca," Lacanian Ink, no. 1, 1991.

1991

De Bruyn, Eric, "Guillermo Kuitca/Julio Galan: Witte de With/Barbara Farber," Artscribe, March/April 1991. pp. 78 - 79.

Greenlees, Donald, "How to Map the Universe," Artnews, October 1991. p. 94 - 95.

Liebmann, Lisa, "Kuitca," The New Yorker, 7 October 1991. p. 13.

Metropolis, (Berlin and New York: Martin Gropius Bau and Rizzoli International Publications, 1991) Edited by Christos Joachimides and Norman Rosenthal.

Mito y Magia en America, Los '80s, (Monterrey, Mexico: Museo de Arte Contemporaneo, 1991) "The Gathering of the Birds," by Francesco Pellizzi.

Newhall, Edith, "A Map of the World," New York Magazine," 30 September 1991. p. 72.

Shaw, Edward, "Guillermo Kuitca's Labor of Love," Buenos Aires Herald, 21 July 1991.

Kuitca, (New York: Annina Nosei Gallery, 1991) text by Aquille Bonito Oliva.

Guillermo Kuitca/Projects 30, (New York: The Museum of Modern Art, 1991) text by Lynn Zelevansky.

McCullough, Ed., "Road Maps of Argentina," Buenos Aires Herald, October 20, 1991.

Russell, Taylor John, "Berlin: The emperor's new wardrobe," The Times, (London), April 26, 1991.

1992

Cuerpo Ausente, (Nantes, France: Musee des Beaux-arts de Nantes, 1992) text by Fabian Lebenglik.

Guillermo Kuitca, (Newport Beach, CA: Newport Harbor Museum, 1992) text by Lynn Zelevansky.

Documenta IX. Kassel, (Stuttgart: Edition Cantz in association with Harry N. Abrams, Inc., New York, 1992) 3 volumes.

Alspaugh, Leann Davis, "Mapping Out a Dream, the Art of Guillermo Kuitca," Museum & Arts, Houston, July 1992. pp. 16 - 17.

Artistas Latinoamericano del siglo XX, (Sevilla, Spain: Comisaria de la Ciudad de Sevilla para 1992 and New York; The Museum of Modern Art, 1992) essay by Edward J. Sulivan.

Johnson, Patricia, "Rooms with a view," The Houston Chronicle, August 8, 1992. pp. 1C and 4C.

Shaw, Edward, "Guillermo Kuitca and his workshop for emerging painters," Buenos Aires Herald, May 11, 1992.

Zaya, Antonio, "Artistas latinoamericanos del siglo XX," Atlantica, Internacional Revista de Las Artes, numero 4, November 1992.

pp. 60 - 65 (Spanish), pp. 119 - 121 (English)

1993

"Art map created especially for this issue of Interview by Guillermo Kuitca," Interview, February 1993. p.127.

"Guillermo Kuitca," Guiarte, Guia Mensual de Las Artes, Madrid, Ano 1, no. 2, Febrero 1993. p. 15 and cover

Un Libro Sobre Guillermo Kuitca, (Amsterdam: Contemporary Art Foundation Amsterdam, and Valencia: IVAM Institut Valencia d'Art Modern, 1993) Essays by Jerry Saltz, Martin Rejtman, Marcelo E. Pacheco.

Guillermo Kuitca, Les Lieux de l'errance, (Montreal, Quebec, Canada: Musee d'Art Contemporain de Montreal, 1993) text by Real Lussier. (brochure)

Guillermo Kuitca. (New York: Sperone Westwater, 1993)

"Goings on About Town," The New Yorker, May 10, 1993. p. 20.

Kimmelman, Michael, "Guillermo Kuitca," The New York Times, Friday, May 14, p. C26.

"Goings on About Town," The New Yorker, May 24, 1993. p. 15.

Smith, Roberta, "20th-Century Latin American Works at the Modern," The New York Time, Friday, June 4, 1993. p. C32.

"Prints & Photographs Published: Guillermo Kuitca," The Print Collector's Newsletter, Vol.XXIV, No.3, July-August. p. 109.

Pini, Ivonne, "Guillermo Kuitca," ArtNexus, July/August 1993. (Columbia) pp. 9 & cover (trans: p. 169.)

Jimenez, Carlos, "Guillermo Kuitca, Un pintor teatral," ArtNexus, July/August 1993 (Columbia) pp. 48 - 51 (trans: pp. 172 - 173.)

Drawing the Line Against AIDS, (USA: The American Foundation for AIDS Research, 1993)

Fernande, Horacio, "A Journey Through The IVAM," ARte COntemporaneo, Report ARCO'93. Preview ARCO'94, Junio 1993. pp. 112 - 118.

Latin American Artists of the Twentieth Century, (New York: The Museum of Modern Art, 1993) edited by Waldo Rasmussen.

Latin American Artists of the Twentieth Century - A Selection from the Exhibition, (New York: The Museum of Modern Art, 1993)

Dona, Lydia, "Guillermo Kuitca Interview," Journal of Contemporary Art, Vol. 6, no. 1, Summer 1993. pp. 56 - 63.

Saltz, Jerry, "Critic's Diary: Mayday, Mayday, Mayday," Art in America, September, pp. 41 - 45. (Kuitca, pp. 43 - 44).

Amor, Monica, "Guillermo Kuitca, Sperone Westwater," ArtNexus, No. 56, Sept-Dec.(Columbia) pp. 144 - 145. (trans: pp. 213-214.)

Zabalbeascoa, Anatxu, "Guillermo Kuitca: IVAM," Artforum, November, p. 117.

Ayerza, Josefina, "Guillermo Kuitca, On the Map," FlashArt, Vol. XXVI, no. 173, November /December, International Edition. pp. 45 - 47.

Living With Art: The Collection of Ellyn & Saul Dennison, (Morristown, NJ: The Morris Museum, 1993)

Arriola, Magali, "guillermo kuitca," poliester, vol. 2, num. 7, fall 1993. pp. 36 - 39.

Leffingwell, Edward, "Latin Soliloquies," Art in America, December. pp. 72 - 83.

1994

Berger, Laurel, "Spotlight: Carmen Alborch, "I'm Not That Predictable," Artnews, February 1994. pp. 53-54.

Horton, Anne, "Kuitca at Sperone Westwater," Art & Auction, May 1994. pp. 84 & 86.

Guillermo Kuitca: The Tablada Suite, (New York: Sperone Westwater, 1994)

Filler, Martin, "Slightly Stateless, but at Home With Himself," The New York Times, May 8, 1994. p. 34H.

Rubinstein, Raphael, "Report from Mexico, Catching the Trade Winds," Art in America, May 1994. pp. 36 - 41 and 43. illus: Guillermo Kuitca installation, mixed mediums; at the Museo de Monterrey, color

Smith, Roberta, "Guillermo Kuitca", The New York Times, Friday, 27 May. p. C24

Steinmetz, Klaus, "Las subastas de noviembre en Sotheby's y Christie's," ArtNexus, No. 12, Abril - Junio 1994. pp. 96 - 97. (Spanish text, translation: pp. 175 - 176) illus: "Sin titulo (Minsk)", color

Choon, Angela, "Openings: Guillermo Kuitca," Art & Antiques, May 1994. p. 34. illus: "Untitled", b/w

"MoMA News and Exhibitions," Flash Art, Vol. XXVII, no. 177, Summer 1994, p. 37.

Cameron, Dan, "Critical Edge," Art & Auction, September 1994, pp. 56, 58, 60

Saltz, Jerry, " A Year in the Life: Tropic of Painting," Art in America, October, 1994, Vol.82, No. 10, pp. 90- 101

Exhibition

Organization
Contemporary Art Foundation Amsterdam

Curator
Eduardo Lipschutz-Villa

Coordination
Sabien Ebeling Koning

Venues
Wexner Center for the Arts,
Columbus, Ohio
Center for Fine Arts,
Miami, Florida
Whitechapel Art Gallery,
London, United Kingdom
Tel Aviv Museum of Art,
Tel Aviv, Israel

Transport
Transport Consultants International Inc.

Publication

Concept
Contemporary Art Foundation Amsterdam

Coordination
Sabien Ebeling Koning
Meghan Ferrill
Jesse Gordon

Text
Josefina Ayerza
Donald Baechler
Douglas Blau
John Coffey
Lynne Cooke
Lelia Driben
Martin Filler
Jesús Fuenmayor
Sherri Geldin
Louis Grachos
Nehama Guralnik
Marvin Heiferman
Anne Horton
Catherine Lampert
Fabián Lebenglik
Lisa Liebmann
Eduardo Lipschutz-Villa
Marc Mayer
Charles Merewether
Miguel Miguel
Edith Newhall
Marcelo Pacheco
Alan Pauls
Robert Rainwater
Kate Rawlinson
Martin Rejtman
Sarah Rogers
Robert Rosenblum
Alisa Tager
Richard Tuttle
Jerry Saltz
Allan Schwartzman
Edward Shaw
Ray Smith
Edward Sullivan
Meyer Vaisman
Matthew Weinstein
Lynn Zelevansky

Cover
Eduardo Lipschutz-Villa
Executed by Hens Breet
for Realitycheck New York

Design
Realitycheck New York

Transcription
Grant Nodine

Translation
Maricruz Smith

Prepress
Hens Breet
Michael Guralnik

Printing
Maxcon Tech/Philips

Photography
*All photograph courtesies are with
the respective galleries and institutes*
Gustavo Lowry
Claudio Gonzales Landa
Dick Loesch

22000M (2.2G)
MADE IN THE U.S.A.